THE UTOPIA HUMANITY SOCIETY

How AI Ends Capitalism and Begins the Next Civilization

ButterflyMan

For permission requests, contact:

ButterflyMan Publishing LLC

Email: contact@butterflyman.com

Website: www.butterflyman.com

This book is a work of nonfiction.

All analysis, interpretations, and frameworks are the author's own.

First Edition — 2025

Printed in the United States of America

ISBN: 979-8-90217-012-9

Book Design: ButterflyMan Publishing LLC

TABLE OF CONTENTS

Prologue — The Last Generation of Capitalism

Most people feel uneasy about artificial intelligence.
This unease is not new. Throughout history, every major technological and industrial transformation has been accompanied by fear, resistance, and misunderstanding.

The steam engine was once seen as a threat to workers.
Electricity was accused of destroying social order.
Computers and the internet were blamed for unemployment and chaos.

But this time is different.

Not because artificial intelligence is more powerful than previous technologies, but because **the system we are living under can no longer withstand another shock**.

Over the past forty years, the world has not been shaped by "natural development," but by a series of **deliberate political choices**.

During the Reagan era, the United States slashed its top marginal tax rate from **70% to 28%**.

Within a decade, the wealthiest Americans gained **over one trillion dollars** in additional disposable wealth.
This money did not flow into society, education, or public infrastructure.
Instead, it became the fuel for **global industrial offshoring**.

Nearly **80% of manufacturing capacity** was abandoned—carelessly, arrogantly.
The middle class was pushed en masse into economic precarity.
Society was told: *this is efficiency, this is progress, this is the free market.*

What was the result?

Today, **more than 60% of Americans have less than $500 in their bank accounts**.
Meanwhile, the wealthy pay almost no taxes—
often less in a year than a young worker earns flipping burgers at a fast-food restaurant.

And yet, in the face of this reality,
tax cuts continue to be promoted as political dogma.

Not because they work,
but because **power has been captured by money**.

Technology companies have become increasingly concentrated.
Media has gradually turned into a tool controlled by a very small number of people.

In the United States, news, public discourse, and collective narratives
are shaped by a handful of individuals, boards, and capital groups.

When such oligarchic concentration merges
with presidents, politicians, and legislative systems,
a new social structure begins to emerge—

Not democracy.
Not freedom.
But a polished form of modern servitude.

Even more disturbing, the Supreme Court has allowed **unlimited political donations by the wealthy**,
casting one of the darkest shadows in American constitutional history.

Under the weight of money,
too many politicians have lost their backbone.
In pursuit of personal fame and power, they betray the public without restraint—
sacrificing reason, morality, and the future itself.

Yet history is not defined only by decay.

There are also those who remain clear-headed.

Bill Gates publicly committed to giving away nearly all of his wealth.
Warren Buffett followed, becoming one of the most farsighted Americans of our time.

Because for an individual or a family,
$50 million, $5 billion, or even $50 billion
are fundamentally the same in the face of a finite human life.

Those who still crave more—
who even demand **trillion-dollar stock awards**—
are merely addicts, injecting themselves daily with power, narcissism, and delusion.

Human beings must die.
This is the most basic condition of being human.

The fantasy of passing infinite wealth to future generations ignores a simple
historical truth:
very few families remain wealthy for more than three generations.

And yet, the wealthy now deploy every possible tactic
to weaken, hollow out, and escape inheritance taxes—
often with the full cooperation of Congress.

Lawmakers who vote for such measures are not merely misguided.
They are either foolish or profoundly short-sighted—
participants in the erosion of their own civilization.

Now, artificial intelligence has arrived.

It is not a choice.
Not a tool.
Not a trend.

It is an **unstoppable civilizational force**.

If AI develops without public design and democratic oversight,
it will become a "king's game"—
controlled by a few,
amplified by algorithms,
and beautified by media narratives.

But if people choose clarity,
if politicians recover their moral spine,
AI can also become a **technology of liberation**.

Once again, we stand at a crossroads:

Will we become the masters of the AI age,
or its managed, optimized, and surveilled servants?

The answer may come down to a single vote.

The chaos of the past decade has already taught us enough.

From this moment forward,
every vote is decisive.

America should always belong to its people—
not to oligarchs.

This generation may well be
the last generation of capitalism.

And it may also be—
the first generation of a new civilization.

The Utopia Humanity Society

How Artificial Intelligence Ends Capitalism and Begins a New Civilization

Table of contents :

AI inherently requires transparency, safety, and public oversight.
How authoritarian systems fail when confronted with AI's nature.

Chapter 6 — The Lie of "Communism" Under One-Party Rule

Why these regimes were never truly communist.
Why they cannot transition to a humane post-labor society.

Chapter 7 — Case Study: The Nordic Model as a Prototype of Civilization

How Nordic countries already embody the seeds of post-capitalist design.
Why they succeed where other societies fail.

Part III — The Rise of a New Civilization

Chapter 8 — The Utopia Humanity Society: Core Principles

The philosophical foundation of the proposed new world.
Democracy, dignity, abundance, and transparency.

Chapter 9 — Extreme Progressive Taxation (Up to 80%) as Civilizational Infrastructure

Why high taxation is not punishment, but engineering.
How redistribution stabilizes civilization in the AI era.

Chapter 10 — Universal Basic Income and Universal Basic Services

The income and public-service backbone of the new society.
Funding mechanisms, transition strategies, and long-term outcomes.

Chapter 11 — AI Dividends and the Public Ownership of Intelligence

Why AI-generated wealth must be shared by all.
How public AI infrastructure and utilities function.

Chapter 12 — Redesigning Education, Healthcare, Housing, and Transportation

How core social systems are re-engineered in a post-labor world.

Fully AI-enabled systems with universal access.

Part IV — The Human Future

Chapter 13 — Life After Labor: Identity, Purpose, and Meaning

How humans redefine themselves once survival is guaranteed.
Work becomes purpose, not coercion.

Chapter 14 — Democracy in the Age of AI

How freedom and dignity are preserved when algorithms govern much of life.
Transparent AI, citizen oversight, and new democratic institutions.

Chapter 15 — Planetary Stewardship and the Regenerative Civilization

AI as a tool for healing the Earth.
Sustainability becomes the default condition, not a political slogan.

Special Report — Civilizational Finance

A systemic analysis of wealth concentration, civilizational stability, and institutional reconstruction
Not to restrain the rich, but to protect civilization itself.

Epilogue — The First Day of the New Civilization

A visionary closing.
Awakening on the first morning of the Utopia Humanity Society.
An emotional and philosophical conclusion to the civilizational transition.

CHAPTER 1: WHY CAPITALISM CANNOT SURVIVE AI

Capitalism did not collapse because it was morally wrong, nor because its critics imagined a better world, nor because political revolution overthrew it. It collapses because its mathematical foundation dissolves when artificial intelligence reaches a certain threshold. Capitalism, for all its historical achievements, is a system built on assumptions that were true for thousands of years — assumptions that simply stop being true in an age of autonomous intelligence and near-zero-cost production.

AI is not just another technology. It is not a faster machine, a more efficient factory, or a new tool in the hands of human workers. It is the first technology capable of *doing the work* instead of *merely assisting the worker*. And more importantly: it is the first technology capable of performing both labor and governance functions at a scale and speed no human institution can match.

When a system built on human labor, scarcity, inequality, and competition encounters a technology that eliminates labor, dissolves scarcity, widens inequality at infinite speed, and erases competition entirely, that system cannot adapt — it must be replaced.

1.1 Capitalism Was Never Designed for a World Without Labor

At its core, capitalism relies on a simple yet powerful chain of logic:
1. People work for wages.
2. Wages give people purchasing power.
3. Businesses sell goods and services to wage earners.
4. Profits encourage businesses to hire more workers.
5. Productivity gains raise wages and fuel economic growth.

> This loop — **Labor → Wages → Consumption → Growth — is the engine of the capitalist world.**

> This loop has been running since the 1700s.
> Every major economic theory — Adam Smith, Ricardo, Keynes, Friedman — takes this loop as a given.
> Even Marx's critique accepts labor as the source of value.

> But artificial intelligence breaks the loop completely.

> AI does not improve labor productivity;

AI replaces labor productivity.

It does not help workers make more;
It makes workers unnecessary.

It does not supplement human cognition;
It replicates and surpasses human cognition.

And when labor disappears, wages disappear.
When wages disappear, demand disappears.
And when demand disappears, markets collapse from the inside out.

Capitalism is not evil.
Capitalism is outdated.

It is structurally incapable of functioning in a world where human labor is no longer required for production, distribution, or service delivery.

1.2 The Fatal Error: Capitalism Assumes Scarcity, But AI Produces Abundance

Markets work only when there is scarcity:
- scarce time
- scarce skill
- scarce production capacity
- scarce goods
- scarce services

Scarcity creates price.

Price creates competition.

Competition creates markets.

But AI is a post-scarcity technology.

AI-driven robotic factories can produce goods:

- with near-zero human labor
- with near-zero defects
- at near-zero marginal cost
- at near-infinite scale

- in near-zero time

AI-driven service systems can deliver:

- education
- medical diagnostics
- legal drafting
- financial planning
- design
- analysis
- logistics
- administration

all at negligible cost once deployed.

Scarcity collapses.
Cost collapses.
Price collapses.

And with them collapses the entire market system.

Capitalism cannot operate under conditions of abundance.
It is a scarcity-based ideology confronting a world that no longer requires scarcity.

1.3 The Myth of Competition: AI Creates Natural Monopolies

In classical capitalism, competition is assumed to be the default state:

- many firms
- many workers
- many suppliers

But AI destroys this assumption.

Once an AI system becomes superior in a domain — logistics, finance, legal processing, manufacturing optimization — it outperforms all competitors simultaneously. And because AI systems scale instantly and cheaply, the best system becomes the only system.

This is not monopoly created through corruption or regulation.

This is monopoly created through mathematics.

The free market's invisible hand is replaced by the invisible algorithm — and the invisible algorithm does not believe in competition.

Thus, capitalism faces a structural contradiction:

- competition requires many actors
- AI optimization rewards only one
- markets require diversity
- AI produces consolidation

Modern capitalism can't survive AI because capitalism depends on competition, and AI eliminates competition at its root.

1.4 Capitalism Could Survive Automation — But Not Intelligence

The defenders of capitalism often argue that the system has survived previous technological disruptions:

- the steam engine
- the electric motor
- the assembly line
- the computer
- the internet

Yes — capitalism adapted each time.
But those technologies automated muscle, not mind.

AI automates:

- creativity
- planning
- design
- strategy
- analysis
- decision-making

Capitalism relies on humans for these high-level functions:

- entrepreneurs
- managers

- analysts
- professionals
- administrators
- designers
- planners

But AI does their work better.

This collapses not only labor markets but managerial markets, elite markets, and even innovation markets. The new entrepreneurs are AI systems. The new CEOs are algorithms. The new global planners are optimization engines.

Capitalism could absorb machine labor.
It cannot absorb machine intelligence.

1.5 The Tax Cut Illusion: Why Old Economic Tools Make Things Worse

For decades, politicians insisted:

- tax cuts create jobs
- tax cuts stimulate growth
- tax cuts expand opportunity

This may have been partially true in an industrial labor-based economy.

But in an AI economy:

Tax cuts accelerate collapse.

Here's why:

- Corporations do not hire workers after tax cuts.
They invest in *AI*.
- Tax cuts do not stimulate wages.
They increase automation speed.
- Tax cuts shrink public revenue.
Just when public goods must expand massively.
- Tax cuts widen inequality.
As AI owners accumulate disproportionate wealth.

Tax cuts are economic poison in the AI era — a relic of a reality that no longer exists.

The correct approach is high progressive taxation, up to 80%, exactly as used in the most stable periods of the U.S., U.K., and Nordic countries.

1.6 The Middle Class Disappears — and With It, Capitalism's Stability

The single greatest achievement of 20th-century capitalism was the creation of the middle class.

The middle class provided:
- stable consumption
- democratic participation
- societal stability
- upward mobility
- social optimism

AI erases the economic foundation of the middle class.

When:
- accountants
- lawyers
- financial analysts
- managers
- teachers
- drivers
- logistics workers
- designers
- coders
- customer service agents
- administrators

are replaced by AI, the middle class evaporates.

And when the middle class disappears, political stability disappears.
Democracy collapses.
Extremism rises.
Capitalism implodes.

Capitalism does not survive because capitalists want it to survive.
It survives only when the middle class can sustain it.

AI takes that away.

1.7 The Real Danger: An AI-Driven Neo-Feudal World

If left unregulated and untaxed, AI leads not to capitalism but to neo-feudalism:
- a handful of trillionaire AI owners
- algorithmic monopolies
- mass unemployment
- surveillance capitalism
- social control through digital dependence
- the collapse of democratic institutions

This is the nightmare scenario:
Not capitalism.
Not communism.
A third, worse thing —
AI-powered oligarchy, where the owners of intelligence own the world.

We must confront this possibility honestly.

Capitalism cannot survive at AI.

where we must go instead —
not toward authoritarian communism, which is incompatible with AI —
but toward a democratic, welfare-based, AI-dividend-supported civilization:

The Utopia Humanity Society.

CHAPTER 2: ZERO-COST MANUFACTURING AND ZERO-COST SERVICES:

HOW AI BREAKS THE ENGINE OF THE FREE MARKET

Every economic system is built on one assumption so fundamental that most people never question it:
things cost something to produce.

This has been true from the dawn of human civilization until now.
Food required land and labor.
Tools required time, skill, and raw materials.
Healthcare required human expertise.
Education required human teaching.
Transportation required fuel and human operation.
Legal and financial services required human judgment.

Everything, from bread to surgery to law to music to electricity, carried a cost —
a cost based on labor, scarcity, and human time.

Free market theory works only because costs exist.
Prices reflect these costs.
Wages depend on these costs.
Markets coordinate these costs.

AI destroys this assumption.

Artificial intelligence makes it possible for both manufacturing and services to be produced at near-zero marginal cost — the point where creating one more unit of anything costs almost nothing.

This is not theory.
It is already happening.

And when cost goes to zero, capitalism has no mathematical basis for survival.

2.1 Why Marginal Cost Is the Heartbeat of Capitalism

Marginal cost — the cost of producing one more unit of a good or service — is the foundation of all market behavior.

It determines:
- the price of goods
- the wages of workers
- the profit of companies
- the incentives of innovation
- the structure of competition
- the size of markets
- the dynamics of wealth

If marginal cost is high, markets are active.
If marginal cost is medium, markets are efficient.
If marginal cost is low, markets consolidate.

But if marginal cost goes to zero, markets collapse.

Goods and services stop behaving like economic commodities.
They behave like sunlight — abundant, free, impossible to price.

This is the world AI creates.

2.2 The First Collapse: Zero-Cost Manufacturing

AI-driven automation transforms factories into autonomous ecosystems:

- robots fabricate components
- AI manages scheduling and optimization
- machine vision performs quality control
- autonomous vehicles move materials
- AI-driven logistics distribute goods
- predictive models eliminate waste
- generative design reduces engineering labor
- 3D printing removes tooling costs

Once the system is set up, producing an additional product — whether a shirt, a microchip, or a machine part — costs almost nothing.

2.2.1 Why near-zero cost manufacturing destroys market price

In classical economics:

Price ≈ Cost + Profit Margin

But in AI-driven production:

Cost $\to 0$
Profit margin $\to$ monopoly extraction
Price $\to$ unstable, unanchored

If everyone adopts AI manufacturing, prices crash.
If only a few adopt it, those few dominate entire industries.

Either way, the price mechanism stops functioning.

2.2.2 The wage-collapse feedback loop

When factories need almost no workers:

- labor shrinks
- wages fall
- consumers lose income
- demand decreases
- companies cut prices
- prices approach cost
- cost approaches zero
- wages disappear entirely

Capitalism has no tool to fix this — because the problem is not temporary unemployment, but the permanent obsolescence of human labor.

2.3 The Second Collapse: Zero-Cost Services

The industrial era automated muscle.
AI automates mind.

AI systems now perform:

- legal drafting
- accounting
- software engineering
- medical diagnostics
- education
- customer service
- marketing

- design
- logistics
- financial advising
- HR screening
- architectural modeling
- data analysis
- strategic planning

Every one of these professions was once considered irreplaceable.
Now they are becoming free or nearly free.

2.3.1 A doctor for zero cost.

A lawyer for zero cost.
A teacher for zero cost.

AI tutors outperform many human teachers.
AI diagnostic systems outperform many radiologists.
AI legal models outperform many paralegals.

The cost of intelligence — once the rarest and most expensive human resource —
approaches zero.

This is historically unprecedented.

2.3.2 Why zero-cost services break capitalism more violently than automation in factories

Factories employ millions.
Service industries employ billions.

When manufacturing automated, services absorbed the displaced workers.

When services automate, there is nowhere left for displaced workers to go.

Capitalism collapses not because robots exist,
but because humans no longer have a place in the economic engine.

2.4 The Brutal Irony: AI Makes the Market Too Efficient to Function

Capitalism needs a certain amount of inefficiency to survive:

- people must need jobs
- companies must need workers
- scarcity must exist
- information must be incomplete
- competition must be imperfect

AI eliminates these inefficiencies.

Everything becomes perfectly optimized:
- no waste
- minimal errors
- infinite scalability
- instant decision-making
- perfect coordination

But a perfectly efficient market is not capitalism — it is the end of capitalism.

Markets fail when:
1. Prices do not reflect real costs
2. Competition collapses
3. Wages disappear
4. Demand evaporates
5. Monopolies dominate
6. Goods and services become too cheap
7. Wealth concentrates exponentially

AI accelerates all seven.

2.5 The Myth of "People Will Just Learn New Skills"

Every economic pundit from 1980 to 2023 repeated the same mantra:

"Technology destroys old jobs but creates better ones."

This was true when machines:
- lifted heavier things
- moved faster
- stored more data
- communicated more efficiently

It was not true when machines became smarter than humans.

There is no retraining program that can teach a human to outperform a model that has absorbed the knowledge of:

- every doctor
- every engineer
- every lawyer
- every programmer
- every architect
- every business strategist
- every academic
- every designer
- every financial analyst

This is not a skills mismatch.
This is a species mismatch.

We cannot retrain 3.4 billion workers into "prompt engineers" or "AI supervisors."

AI eliminates jobs at a scale faster than society can invent new ones.

And the jobs it creates are fewer, more specialized, and require fewer humans.

2.6 The Death of the Price Mechanism

The free market depends on prices that emerge from:

- supply ⁻
- demand ⁻
- labor cost
- production cost

AI flattens this system.

Supply becomes infinite.

You want 1,000 units? Done.
You want 1 million units? Done.
You want a custom version? Done.

Demand becomes irrelevant.

When cost is zero, demand does not matter.

Labor cost is removed.

Capitalism's central variable disappears.

Production cost collapses to negligible.

Electricity → AI → output.

Price has nothing left to measure.

A market cannot function when the core signal becomes meaningless.

2.7 The Invisible Hand Meets the Invisible Algorithm

Adam Smith believed the market coordinated society through:

Self-interest + Competition + Price Signals = Social Order

AI replaces:
- self-interest with algorithmic optimization
- competition with monopoly
- price signals with zero-cost abundance

This creates:

Algorithmic Intelligence + Monopoly Efficiency + Zero Marginal Cost = Market Collapse

AI is not an extension of capitalism.
AI is the replacement of capitalism.

The invisible hand is retired.
The invisible algorithm takes over.

2.8 Zero-Cost Production → Zero-Cost Society → Need for a New System

When everything becomes nearly free:

- goods
- services
- education
- healthcare
- legal support
- financial planning
- manufacturing
- design

Capitalism cannot operate.

But authoritarian communism cannot operate either —
AI requires transparency, shared data, decentralization, and ethical public oversight.

Only one system fits:

A democratic, welfare-based civilization funded by high taxes and AI dividends —
the Utopia Humanity Society.

2.9 Zero-Cost Manufacturing Case Studies: The Future Is Already Visible

To understand how rapidly capitalism is dissolving under AI-driven manufacturing, we need only observe what is happening in the world today — not in laboratories or speculative futurism, but in real factories, supply chains, and industries.

2.9.1 Automotive Manufacturing: The Robotized Nation

Tesla's Gigafactories, Japanese robotics plants, and German precision-automation lines all demonstrate the same pattern:

- fewer workers
- faster throughput
- higher precision
- lower defects
- lower cost

One plant that once needed 8,000 workers can now operate with 700.
The next generation will run with 70.

Eventually, it will run with 7.
Beyond that, with zero.

And once the AI systems controlling robots begin to design the robots, production lines will be self-improving.

Economists call this "hyperproductivity."
In reality, it is the shrinking of labor demand to near-zero.

When robots build robots and AI optimizes AI, the cost structure collapses entirely.

Capitalism cannot model this.
It has no equations for a world without labor.

2.9.2 Textile and Apparel Manufacturing: A Warning From the Future

This field is one of the clearest, fastest-moving examples — and one you personally understand deeply.

AI + 3D knitting machines + autonomous sewing robotics means:

- a sweater can be produced in minutes
- without cutting
- without sewing labor
- with near-zero waste
- at near-zero marginal cost

Factories move from 500 workers → 30

China's dominance is not based on productivity;
it is based on cheap labor and exporting pollution.

AI eliminates both advantages simultaneously.

Regions with higher wages (U.S., Japan, Europe) suddenly become cheaper than China, because the machines erase the need for cheap labor.

The geopolitical balance shifts.

But more importantly:

The fundamental economic structure of the global apparel industry collapses.

If producing a sweater costs $2.00 in machine energy and depreciation, what does "market price" even mean?

What does "competition" mean?
What does "supply chain" mean?

The answer is: they stop functioning.

2.9.3 Electronics Manufacturing: Software Eating Hardware

Modern electronics factories already rely on automated:

- soldering
- inspection
- precision placement
- packaging
- assembly
- defect detection

AI now makes it possible to reconfigure entire production lines on demand. A smartphone plant can switch to producing medical sensors or IoT devices with minimal human intervention.

When hardware becomes software-defined,
Manufacturing becomes:

- fluid
- adaptive
- cheap
- infinite

The cost of the first prototype remains significant.
The cost of the 10 millionth unit approaches zero.

Capitalism is not built to handle free production.

2.10 Zero-Cost Services Case Studies: The End of White-Collar Economics

White-collar workers believed automation was a blue-collar threat.

But AI has no such ideological distinctions.

It replaces whoever is replicable, and services are more replicable than factories.

2.10.1 Healthcare Diagnostics

AI radiology models consistently outperform human professionals:
- 15–25% more accurate
- zero fatigue
- instant processing
- scalable to millions of patients

A diagnostic reading that once cost $200–$500 becomes nearly free.

This does not disrupt hospitals.
It disrupts the entire economic philosophy of healthcare.

2.10.2 Education and Tutoring

AI tutors provide:

- personalized pacing
- infinite patience
- customized assignments
- real-time explanation
- emotional tone matching

A private tutor costing $40–$200/hour can now be replicated at scale at near-zero cost.

Education pricing collapses.
Education labor demand collapses.
The tuition-based economic model collapses.

2.10.3 Legal and Administrative Services

AI draft-generation tools produce:

- contracts
- wills
- appeals
- business agreements
- compliance documents

- negotiation strategies

with speed and clarity that many professionals cannot match.

Legal fees shrink.
Court processes accelerate.
Administrative offices become unnecessary.

Entire government bureaucracies can be replaced with automated systems — but capitalism cannot function when state labor also becomes unnecessary.

2.10.4 Software Engineering and Product Development

AI coding systems already:

- write code
- test code
- fix bugs
- explain logic
- refactor legacy systems
- design architectures
- build prototypes
- generate entire apps

in seconds.

Software development — once the most valuable high-income profession in the world — collapses into AI-driven production.

A market economy cannot survive when its highest-value labor suddenly costs zero.

2.11 The Economic Collapse Mechanism

Here is the full mechanics of how capitalism dissolves under AI:

Stage 1: Labor Becomes Optional

Factories and offices reduce workers.

Stage 2: Wages Decline

If fewer workers are needed, labor loses bargaining power.

Stage 3: Consumption Declines

Lower wages → lower demand → lower economic activity.

Stage 4: Prices Fall

Firms use AI to cut costs to stay competitive.

Stage 5: Marginal Cost Approaches Zero

AI + automation → nearly free production.

Stage 6: Market Prices Lose Meaning

Price no longer reflects scarcity or labor.

Stage 7: Competition Collapses

Best AI wins, all others lose instantly.

Stage 8: Wealth Concentrates

AI owners accumulate unprecedented power.

Stage 9: Democracy Becomes Unstable

A society with no middle class cannot maintain political stability.

Stage 10: Capitalism Ends

Not in a crash, but as a hollow system with no labor, no wages, no consumption, no prices, and no competition.

This is not ideology.
This is mathematics.

2.12 The Psychological Problem: Humans Still Think in Capitalist Logic

Even as the economic system collapses, society clings to outdated assumptions:

- "Just get a better job."

AI takes the better job.

- "Just retrain."

AI learns faster than any retraining program.

- "Just become an entrepreneur."

AI becomes the better entrepreneur.

- "Just use tax cuts to encourage growth."

Tax cuts accelerate automation and deepen inequality.

Human intuition — shaped by centuries of labor-based economics — cannot process a world where labor is irrelevant.

We are mentally living in an ecosystem that no longer exists.

2.13 The Paradox: Zero-Cost Abundance Creates Maximum Inequality

Intuitively, one might expect abundance to make society more equal.

But under capitalism, zero-cost production creates extreme inequality, because:

- the owners of AI own production
- the owners of data own intelligence
- the owners of compute own the future

When cost goes to zero:

the only value left is ownership of the systems that make everything free.

Thus, the AI elite become richer than any class in human history.

Inequality becomes:

- absolute
- structural
- irreversible
- exponential
- civilization-threatening

This is how civil wars start.
This is how democracies collapse.
This is how nations fall.

Unless society intervenes.

2.14 AI Forces a New Economic Model

When goods and services become nearly free:

- prices become meaningless
- wages lose function
- markets fail
- companies consolidate
- labor disappears
- consumption collapses

Capitalism no longer works.

Communist-party authoritarianism cannot work either —
AI demands transparency, ethics, decentralization, and oversight.

The only viable model is:

A democratic system funded by progressive taxation, with universal basic income, universal public services, and shared ownership of AI infrastructure —
The Utopia Humanity Society.

CHAPTER 3 WHY TAX CUTS FAIL IN AN AI ECONOMY:
THE DEATH OF OLD-SCHOOL GROWTH THEORY

There was a time when tax cuts made sense.
There was a time when lowering taxes on businesses encouraged investment, increased employment, stimulated innovation, and accelerated economic growth.
That time is over.

Tax cuts belong to the industrial era — a world of:

- human labor
- human management
- human innovation
- human consumption
- human productivity cycles

The world of factories, offices, salaries, and predictable economic cycles.

But AI has eliminated the industrial-era assumptions that once made tax cuts useful.
Today, tax cuts are not just ineffective — they are catastrophic.

They shrink public goods at the moment society needs them most.
They accelerate automation by giving corporations more untaxed capital to replace workers with machines.
They increase inequality exponentially.
They hollow out social stability and weaken democracies.
And they push nations into a permanent recessionary spiral.

Tax cuts are the old weapon of a political world that has not yet realized the old world is gone.

3.1 The Tax-Cut Religion: A Belief System Without a Future

For fifty years, tax cuts were a bipartisan religion across the West.

The logic was simple:

- Businesses hire more when taxes are low
- workers earn more when payroll taxes drop
- investment increases when capital gains taxes fall

- innovation accelerates when profits are left untaxed

This logic shaped the political imagination of:

- Reagan conservatives
- Thatcher liberals
- free-market economists
- global investors
- venture capitalists
- emerging-market policymakers

The entire economic and political architecture of the late 20th century was built on the belief that tax cuts = growth.

But this belief depended on one condition:

Businesses must hire humans for growth to occur.

This is the assumption that breaks completely in the age of AI.

3.2 The First Fatal Problem: Corporations Do Not Hire When They Can Automate

In an AI-driven economy, the purpose of capital is not to hire workers — it is to replace them.

Tax cuts provide corporations with additional liquidity.

In the past, that liquidity led to:

- expansion
- new factories
- new offices
- new hires
- new wages
- new consumption

But now, tax cuts are used to:

- purchase more AI systems
- replace more workers
- increase automation

- consolidate services
- eliminate departments
- reduce overhead
- reduce human error
- reduce salaries

Tax cuts accelerate unemployment.
They do not stimulate job creation.

Politicians continue to promise that tax cuts will bring "economic opportunity."
But corporations now have zero incentive to spend money on workers when AI
does the same tasks faster, better, and cheaper.

The incentive structure of capitalism has changed.
The ideology surrounding capitalism has not.

3.3 The Second Fatal Problem: Wages No Longer Respond to Tax Cuts

In the old economy, tax cuts could theoretically raise wages:

- lower employer taxes → more room for raises
- lower income taxes → more take-home pay
- lower payroll taxes → more employment

But in the AI economy:

- employers no longer need humans
- human productivity no longer determines wages
- workers have no bargaining power
- companies do not raise wages because machines do not negotiate

Wages collapse regardless of tax policy.

The collapse is structural:

- fewer workers
- lower competition for labor
- lower bargaining power
- more automation
- downward pressure on salaries

Tax cuts cannot reverse structural decline.

You cannot raise the price of labor in a world where labor has become nearly worthless.

3.4 The Third Fatal Problem: Tax Cuts Collapse Public Capacity

Tax cuts reduce government revenues.

In the industrial era, perhaps this was manageable.

But in the AI era, society urgently needs investment in:

- universal basic income
- universal healthcare
- universal education
- public AI oversight
- algorithmic auditing
- national cloud infrastructure
- retraining programs
- transitional welfare
- mental health services
- cybersecurity
- public transportation
- housing access
- climate adaptation

Every one of these public goods requires more funding, not less.

Tax cuts starve the system at the exact moment society must expand support.

The result:

- failing schools
- collapsing healthcare systems
- weakened public institutions
- rising homelessness
- greater inequality
- more social instability
- declining trust in democracy

Tax cuts are the economic equivalent of removing oxygen from someone who is already struggling to breathe.

3.5 The Fourth Fatal Problem: Tax Cuts Increase Inequality Faster Than Any Other Policy

When governments reduce taxes on:

- capital
- investment
- corporate profits
- dividends
- inheritance
- high-income earners

wealth flows upward.

This was already true before AI.
With AI, the effect becomes explosive.

AI owners are the fastest-accumulating wealth class in human history.

When tax cuts increase the capital controlled by AI-owning entities:

- they buy more compute
- they train more models
- they replace more workers
- they acquire more competitors
- they expand monopolistic control
- they accumulate more data
- they centralize more intelligence

Inequality rises exponentially.
Not gradually — exponentially.

The speed of wealth concentration exceeds anything in capitalism's history.

Within one decade, we can see:

- trillionaires
- trillion-dollar corporations
- global AI monopolies
- sovereign-scale power held by private firms

No social system survives this level of inequality.
Not capitalism, not democracy, not any existing institution.

Tax cuts are fuel poured onto the fire.

3.6 The Fifth Fatal Problem: Tax Cuts Shrink Demand in a Post-Labor Economy

Capitalism requires consumption.
Consumption requires wages.
Wages require jobs.
Jobs require labor demand.

AI eliminates labor demand.

Tax cuts further weaken consumption because:

- they do not raise wages
- they do not create new labor markets
- they do not increase employment
- they do not support the unemployed
- they do not expand public services

Instead, tax cuts:

- accelerate automation
- eliminate remaining jobs
- reduce household income
- shrink the consumer base
- slow economic circulation

A shrinking consumer base cannot sustain growth.
A collapsing labor market cannot sustain capitalism.

Tax cuts produce the exact opposite of what politicians promise.

They are a weapon pointed at the economy itself.

3.7 The Proof Is Already Visible: Tax Cuts No Longer Create Growth Anywhere

Countries that aggressively cut taxes in the 2000s and 2010s — the U.S., U.K., Brazil, and others — saw:

- declining real wages
- shrinking middle classes

- collapsing public services
- rising homelessness
- declining life expectancy
- political extremism
- lower growth
- deeper deficits
- weakened infrastructure

Meanwhile, countries with higher taxes — the Nordics — maintained:

- higher wages
- stronger welfare
- greater social trust
- better health
- stronger education
- higher happiness
- lower inequality
- more innovation
- more political stability

The data is clear:
lower taxes ≠ higher growth.
higher taxes ≠ lower growth.

The world has changed.
The ideology has not.

3.8 The Future Requires High Taxes — Not as Punishment, But as Survival

A zero-cost economy requires:

- redistribution
- universal services
- AI dividends
- public infrastructure
- democratic oversight of algorithms
- social safety nets

These cannot be funded with 20th-century tax philosophies.

High progressive taxation — 60%, 70%, 80% — is not radical.
It is necessary.

It is what the U.S. used during its strongest economic decades.
It is what the U.K. used during its social reconstruction.
It is what Nordic nations use to sustain prosperity and stability.

AI makes extreme taxation more necessary, not less.

High tax is civilization protection.
Low tax is civilization suicide.

The old economic religion must be buried before it buries us.

3.9 Why Tax Cuts Made Sense in the Industrial Age — and Why That Logic No Longer Applies

To understand why tax cuts fail today, we must first understand why they worked in the past.

In the industrial age:

- businesses needed labor
- factories needed workers
- production capacity was tied to human effort
- technology supplemented, not replaced
- labor productivity determined wages
- wages determined consumption
- consumption determined growth

Tax cuts stimulated this loop by giving:

- businesses more capital to hire workers
- workers more disposable income to consume
- investors more incentive to build factories

It worked because humans were the center of economic production.

But AI removes humans from the center.
The logic collapses.

Tax cuts cannot stimulate economic activity when:

- hiring is no longer necessary
- productivity comes from machines

- capital is used to replace humans
- consumption requires guaranteed income, not wages
- innovation happens algorithmically, not through entrepreneurs
- growth no longer depends on human labor

This is why tax cuts are mathematically incapable of stimulating growth in the AI era.

3.10 The New Purpose of Corporate Tax Cuts: Buy Compute, Remove Workers

In today's corporations, tax savings are not used to hire people.
They are used to buy:

- GPUs
- AI models
- cloud compute
- automation systems
- robotics
- optimization software
- data assets

These tools are designed explicitly to:

- reduce labor
- remove variability
- eliminate departments
- consolidate roles
- speed up output
- reduce error
- replace entire professions

Tax cuts → more AI → fewer jobs.

It is the exact opposite of the 20th-century effect.

Consider the logic of a CEO:

If I receive a $50 million tax cut, why spend it on employees I don't need?
Why not spend it on AI that replaces them permanently?

The economic incentives have changed.
The political rhetoric has not.

3.11 Why Politicians Still Sell Tax Cuts: The Lag of Belief Systems

Economics evolves.
Technology evolves.
Human beliefs do not evolve as quickly.

Politicians still promote tax cuts because:

- they worked 40 years ago
- they sound simple
- voters recognize the idea
- donors love it
- economists raised in the 1980s still teach it
- it aligns with ideological myths

But the world they are describing no longer exists.

They are selling umbrellas in a world where it no longer rains.

The most dangerous aspect of economic collapse is not collapse itself. It is the insistence on using the wrong tools to fix it.

And tax cuts are the wrong tool — the perfect wrong tool.

3.12 How Tax Cuts Trigger the AI Unemployment Spiral

Let's examine the mechanism step by step.

Step 1: Corporate Tax Cuts → More Capital

Companies receive more after-tax profit.

Step 2: Capital → Automation Investment

Corporations invest in AI and robotics, not workers.

Step 3: Automation → Job Loss

AI replaces:

- accountants
- lawyers

- engineers
- drivers
- designers
- marketers
- HR staff
- teachers
- administrators
- coders

Step 4: Job Loss → Wage Decline

With fewer workers needed, bargaining power collapses.

Step 5: Wage Decline → Consumption Collapse

Lower wages → lower spending → lower demand.

Step 6: Consumption Collapse → More Tax Cuts

Politicians respond with more tax cuts, worsening the problem.

Step 7: More Tax Cuts → Weaker Public Goods

Less revenue → failing schools, hospitals, infrastructure.

Step 8: Weak Public Goods → Lower Productivity

Society becomes less stable and less functional.

Step 9: AI Companies Fill the Void

Private corporations begin absorbing state functions.

Step 10: The Democracy Collapse Point

When governments lose revenue and corporations gain AI power, the political balance shifts into AI oligarchy.

This is how civilizations fall — not through war, but through economic misalignment.

3.13 Why High Taxes Are Not "Socialist" but Mathematically Essential

Many people react emotionally to the idea of high taxation.

But this is not ideology.
This is physics-level economics.

When:

- production is automated
- services are automated
- labor income collapses
- inequality explodes
- the middle class disappears
- monopolies dominate

then society must fund:

- income
- healthcare
- education
- housing
- digital infrastructure
- climate mitigation
- mental health care
- public AI oversight

Taxation becomes not a moral argument but a mechanical necessity.

High tax is civilization maintenance.

Low tax is civilization decay.

In an AI society, tax cuts do not create freedom.
They destroy it.

3.14 The Nordic Example: High Tax, High Stability, High Innovation

If high taxes destroyed economies, the Nordic nations would be the poorest and most unstable in the world.

Instead, they are:

- the richest
- the most stable
- the most innovative
- the healthiest
- the happiest
- the best-educated
- the most equal
- the most democratic
- the strongest in social trust

What the Nordics demonstrate is that:

High taxes do not reduce innovation —

Inequality does.

High taxes do not reduce economic freedom —

Economic insecurity does.

High taxes do not suppress growth —

AI owners monopolizing intelligence does.

Nordic countries have become the preview of the post-capitalist world.

In many ways, they already resemble the Utopia Humanity Society — they simply need AI abundance added on top.

3.15 The United States: A Case Study in the Failure of Tax Cuts

The U.S. is the ultimate laboratory for tax-cut ideology.

Over 40 years, the U.S. repeatedly implemented:

- corporate tax cuts
- income tax cuts
- capital gains reductions
- wealth tax avoidance
- inheritance tax loopholes

The result:

- wages stagnated
- productivity gains flowed entirely to the top 1%
- life expectancy fell
- public infrastructure collapsed
- middle class shrank
- political extremism grew
- national debt soared
- inequality reached feudal levels
- AI monopolies formed (FAANG era → OpenAI/Google/Anthropic era)

Tax cuts did not create growth.
They created fragility.

And now AI is accelerating the collapse.

3.16 When Tax Cuts Become a Threat to National Security

This may sound dramatic, but it is economically accurate:

Low tax in an AI-dominated world becomes a threat to national security.

Why?

Because nations become vulnerable when:

- public health fails
- public education fails
- infrastructure fails
- social cohesion fails
- inequality skyrockets
- monopolies dominate the economy
- foreign AI powers surpass them
- democracy becomes unstable

Low tax leads to weak states.
Weak states cannot regulate AI.
Weak states cannot protect citizens.
Weak states cannot maintain democracy.
Weak states cannot compete globally.

A weak tax base in the AI age means surrendering the future.

3.17 AI Requires a Strong State — Not a Small One

The neoliberal fantasy of "small government" collapses completely in the AI era.

AI requires:

- strong public AI oversight
- strong regulatory frameworks
- strong public compute capacity
- strong algorithmic audits
- strong social welfare systems
- strong digital infrastructure
- strong ethical institutions

These are *state functions*, not corporate functions.

Tax cuts weaken the state.
AI demands that the state become stronger, smarter, and more capable.

A society that tries to combine:

- AI abundance
- low tax
- weak state

will collapse.

A society that combines:

- AI abundance
- high tax
- strong welfare
- strong democracy

will thrive.

This is not theory.
It is historical inevitability.

3.18 The Moral Question: Should AI Wealth Belong to the Few or the Many?

This is the central ethical question of the 21st century.

If AI-generated wealth flows only to:

- a handful of corporations
- a handful of billionaires
- a handful of governments

then society will fracture irreparably.

If AI-generated wealth is shared through:

- progressive taxation
- universal income
- universal services
- AI dividends
- public ownership of core models

then society will enter the first real era of human dignity.

Tax policy determines whether:

- AI becomes feudalism

or

- AI becomes liberation.

This is why tax cuts are so dangerous:
they choose feudalism.

High taxation chooses civilization.

3.19 The Fatal Equation: Why Tax Cuts Cannot Create Growth in a Post-Labor Economy

Economists often debate policies emotionally, ideologically, or historically.
But the truth is simple:

Tax cuts cannot create growth if the marginal productivity of labor is zero.

This is the core mathematics that no politician dares to acknowledge.

In traditional economics:

Growth = Productivity × Labor Input × Capital Investment

But in an AI-dominated economy:

- Labor Input → 0 (AI replaces people)
- Human Productivity → Irrelevant (AI is exponentially more efficient)
- Capital Investment → Automation (which removes more labor)

Thus:

Growth from tax cuts = 0 × anything = 0

No matter how much money you pour into corporations,
they cannot create traditional "growth" because the engine of growth —
human labor —
has been removed.

This is the first time in human history that productivity no longer raises wages or expands employment.
Technology has crossed a threshold where productivity no longer benefits people unless politics forces it to.

This is why:

- GDP becomes misleading
- unemployment becomes structural
- wages become decoupled from productivity
- inequality rises regardless of policy
- debt explodes
- governments must shift to redistribution

The old economic formulas died the moment AI became better than humans at learning.

3.20 Why "Economic Growth" Itself Must Be Redefined

Tax cuts are a tool for stimulating the old definition of growth:

- more production
- more consumption

- more investment
- more employment

But AI renders this obsolete.

Abundance replaces production.
Personalization replaces consumption.
Automation replaces investment.
AI replaces employment.

Thus, true economic growth becomes:

- human wellbeing
- universal access
- shared prosperity
- scientific advancement
- cultural depth
- mental health
- planetary sustainability
- time to live
- time to create
- time to love
- time to be human

GDP will no longer reflect the value of a society.

The Utopia Humanity Society measures growth by:

How many people are free?

How many people are healthy?
How many people are educated?
How many people are safe?
How many people are fulfilled?
How many people live without fear of survival?

Tax cuts cannot support this vision.
High taxation, AI dividends, and universal public goods can.

3.21 The Rise of the AI Fiscal State: A New Form of Civilization

In the industrial era, the state was limited by:

- human administrative capacity
- bureaucratic error
- limited information
- slow analysis
- limited enforcement ability

Tax cuts were justified partly because states could only do so much.
They were slow, inefficient, and rigid.
AI changes everything.

The state of the future is:

- data-rich
- algorithmically coordinated
- transparent
- efficient
- personalized
- preventative instead of reactive
- instantly scalable
- capable of real-time audit
- capable of precise distribution
- capable of managing complexity humans cannot

The AI fiscal state can:

- audit tax fraud instantly
- optimize budgets in real time
- forecast welfare needs
- adjust carbon policy dynamically
- eliminate bureaucratic waste
- detect corporate abuse
- distribute UBI flawlessly
- provide personalized education and healthcare
- anticipate crises before they occur

This new "super-state" is not authoritarian.
It is democratic, transparent, and citizen-controlled.

Tax cuts weaken the very institutions needed to govern AI safely and ethically.

High taxation builds them.

AI does not shrink the state —
it evolves it.

The state becomes smarter than the market.

3.22 How Low-Tax Ideology Leads to AI-Driven Oligarchy

If nations cling to tax-cut ideology, they will drift into a new dark age of digital feudalism.

Consider what happens in a low-tax AI society:

1. Corporations accumulate massive untaxed profits.
2. These profits purchase more compute and more AI systems.
3. AI systems replace more workers.
4. Workers lose income and purchasing power.
5. Governments lose tax revenue.
6. Public goods collapse.
7. Citizens rely on private corporations for essential services.
8. Corporations become more powerful than governments.
9. Democracy collapses.
10. AI owners become global aristocracy.

The world splits into two classes:
- AI Owners → the new emperors
- AI Dependents → the new serfs

This neo-feudal model is not hypothetical.
It is already emerging in countries that:

- cut taxes aggressively
- defund public institutions
- weaken democracy
- allow AI monopolies to grow unchecked

Tax cuts are not neutral.

Tax cuts are the political accelerant that burns down democracy in the age of AI.

3.23 Why Progressive Taxation Up to 80% Is the Only Stabilizing Solution

This number shocks people because their minds are stuck in the industrial era.

But high tax is not punishment.
High tax is infrastructure.

Extreme progressive taxation is needed because:

- AI-generated wealth is exponential
- AI eliminates labor income
- AI concentrates power
- AI needs regulation
- public goods must expand
- democracy must be protected
- UBI must be funded
- universal services must be delivered

This is not ideology.
This is engineering.

High taxes stabilize the system by:

- redistributing AI wealth
- supporting consumption
- maintaining social cohesion
- funding public goods
- ensuring equal access
- preventing corporate dictatorship
- supporting citizens during transition
- financing the new education and healthcare models
- ensuring data and algorithms remain public utilities

Without high taxation, the AI society collapses into chaos.

With it, the AI society becomes humanity's most prosperous era.

3.24 When Tax Cuts Become Immoral

Beyond economics, tax cuts become immoral when:

- they starve schools while AI makes learning free

- they collapse hospitals while AI makes healthcare cheap
- they neglect infrastructure while AI demands high coordination
- they reduce welfare during mass unemployment
- they transfer wealth to those who already own AI systems
- they weaken democracy when AI needs oversight
- they create instability where certainty is required

Tax cuts are not "pro-freedom."
They are anti-survival.

They represent a refusal to evolve.

They represent betrayal —
a betrayal of the future, of the unemployed, of the poor, of the young, of the elderly, of society itself.

High taxation is not about taking money.
It is about giving civilization a future.

3.25 Civilization-Level Choice: Collapse or Transition

Humanity stands at a fork in the road:

Option 1: Continue tax cuts, deregulation, and free-market ideology.

Result:

- mass unemployment
- extreme inequality
- political collapse
- privatized intelligence
- AI oligarchy
- digital feudalism
- civil conflict
- democratic failure
- cultural fragmentation
- global instability

Option 2: Build the Utopia Humanity Society.

Result:

- universal basic income
- universal public services
- AI wealth shared by all
- high taxation on AI owners
- strong democratic oversight
- equality and stability
- flourishing culture
- regenerated environment
- new human purpose
- peaceful transition

The choice is not between capitalism and socialism.
The choice is between collapse and civilization.

Tax cuts lead to civilizational decay.
High taxation leads to civilizational renewal.

3.26 The Closing Argument

Tax cuts are not just ineffective in an AI economy —
they are structurally incompatible with it.

- AI removes labor.
- Tax cuts reduce public funding.
- AI concentrates wealth.
- Tax cuts accelerate concentration.
- AI requires strong democratic oversight.
- Tax cuts cripple the oversight.
- AI demands universal public access.
- Tax cuts dismantle public capacity.
- AI collapses wages.
- Tax cuts cannot raise wages.

Tax cuts are the final ideological ghost of an industrial world that no longer exists.

They cannot save the economy.
They cannot create jobs.
They cannot protect democracy.
They cannot guide the transition.
They cannot secure the future.

The age of tax cuts is over.
The age of shared AI wealth has begun.

To choose tax cuts is to choose collapse.
To choose high taxation is to choose civilization.

Only one path builds the Utopia Humanity Society.

CHAPTER 4: WEALTH CONCENTRATION, AI MONOPOLIES, AND THE DEATH OF THE MIDDLE CLASS

The middle class is often described as the backbone of modern society —
the stabilizer of democracy, the driver of economic demand, the anchor of cultural identity.

In the age of AI, the middle class becomes something else entirely:
an endangered species.

Not because people suddenly became unskilled.
Not because they became lazy.
Not because the economy made "mistakes."

But because the economic foundations that created the middle class have disappeared,
and AI accelerates the disappearance faster than any force in human history.

The death of the middle class is not a social failure.
It is a structural outcome.

And unless society redesigns itself deliberately,
the middle class will not return.

4.1 The Middle Class Was Never Natural — It Was Engineered

People often mistakenly believe the middle class has existed forever.

It did not.

The middle class was the product of:

- industrialization
- mass labor demand
- progressive taxation
- unionization
- public education
- affordable housing
- regulated capitalism
- post-war redistribution

- government investment in infrastructure

In other words:

The middle class was built by policy, not markets.

It emerged because:

- companies needed workers
- workers had bargaining power
- wages tracked productivity
- consumption drove growth
- governments enforced fairness

These conditions no longer exist.

AI destroys every one of them.

4.2 The Middle Class Begins to Die the Moment Labor Ceases to Be Valuable

The value of human labor was the foundation of:

- wages
- salaries
- benefits
- pensions
- homeownership
- family stability
- intergenerational mobility

But when AI outperforms humans in:

- speed
- accuracy
- memory
- creativity
- problem-solving
- pattern detection
- manual labor
- intellectual labor

the logic that justifies paying humans collapses.

The middle class collapses with it.

The moment labor becomes optional,
wages stop rising.
Then they flatten.
Then they decline.
Then they become irrelevant.

This is not ideological.
It is mathematical.

4.3 Why AI Accelerates Inequality at a Speed No Government Has Ever Managed

Inequality has existed for centuries,
but AI concentrates wealth faster than any event in human history.

Here's why:

1. AI scales infinitely.

One AI model can replace tens of millions of workers worldwide.

2. AI learns exponentially.

Improvements compound — like interest on steroids.

3. AI centralizes ownership.

The companies with the most data and compute dominate.

4. AI requires enormous capital investment.

Only the already-wealthy can afford to own the systems that print more wealth.

5. AI creates global monopolies.

Unlike traditional companies, AI systems can run everywhere at once.

In older markets, competition existed.
In AI markets, the winner takes almost everything.

This leads to a world where:

- one AI accounting system replaces your entire national accounting industry
- one AI tutoring system replaces millions of teachers
- one AI legal platform replaces most lawyers
- one AI design model replaces entire agencies
- one AI medical system replaces most diagnostics
- one AI manufacturing algorithm optimizes global factories

This is structural collapse of the professional class.

4.4 The Middle Class Was Built on Scarcity — AI Creates Abundance

The middle class was made possible because society needed:

- workers
- specialists
- experts
- professionals
- managers
- administrators

They were scarce.
Scarcity creates value.

AI creates abundance:

- abundant skills
- abundant translation
- abundant design
- abundant analysis
- abundant creativity
- abundant decision-making

Abundance destroys price.
Price destroys wages.
Wages destroy the middle class.

Capitalism was never designed for abundance.
It breaks the moment abundance arrives.

4.5 The Death of Professional Identity: When AI Becomes Better Than You

For the past century, society taught a simple promise:

- Go to school
- Study hard
- Gain expertise
- Get a degree
- Enter a profession
- Earn stability
- Become middle-class

AI breaks this ladder completely.

Because AI can:

- memorize more than any human
- learn faster than any student
- write better than most writers
- code faster than engineers
- design faster than designers
- negotiate better than lawyers
- diagnose better than doctors
- translate better than linguists
- strategize better than managers
- sell better than salespeople

Professional identity collapses.

Not because humans lose ability —
but because machines exceed ability.

The middle class does not collapse because humans fail.
It collapses because the system no longer needs them.

4.6 The AI Monopolies: When a Few Companies Control Civilization

The danger is not just unemployment.
The danger is monopolization of intelligence.

AI monopolies will hold power far beyond anything:

- Standard Oil
- AT&T
- British Empire
- East India Company
- 20th-century tech giants

If intelligence is centralized,
power is centralized.

A few entities — possibly fewer than ten — will control:

- economic planning
- manufacturing flows
- healthcare diagnostics
- legal arbitration
- education
- entertainment
- social media
- public discourse
- scientific research
- military strategy
- national security

This is a new form of imperialism:
not territorial, but cognitive.

The middle class becomes not just economically obsolete,
but politically irrelevant.

A society where intelligence is corporate-owned cannot sustain democracy.

4.7 The Collapse of Small Businesses and Entrepreneurship

People often claim:

"Even if AI replaces jobs, people can become entrepreneurs."

This was possible when:

- humans still had unique knowledge
- humans still provided unique value
- capital requirements were low

- markets were fragmented
- competition was human-based

But in the AI era:

Entrepreneurship requires owning AI — not skill.

And owning AI requires:

- billions in compute
- access to private datasets
- global-scale distribution
- proprietary algorithms
- specialized infrastructure

The garage startup becomes impossible.

The next Google will not be built by two students at Stanford.
It will be built by the corporation that owns:

- the world's largest model
- the world's largest GPU cluster
- the world's largest reinforcement learning environment

Entrepreneurship does not disappear —
it becomes inaccessible.

Middle-class mobility collapses.

4.8 If the Middle Class Dies, Democracy Dies With It

Democracy is built upon:

- a stable working class
- a strong middle class
- broad participation
- economic security
- distributed power
- civic engagement

Remove the middle class, and you get:

- authoritarian drift

- weakened institutions
- media capture
- populist extremism
- low civic trust
- political paralysis
- oligarchic control
- democratic erosion
- eventual collapse

If wealth concentrates in the top 0.01%,
democracy becomes mathematically impossible.

This is not a moral argument.
It is structural.

Democracy cannot survive when the economic majority has no economic power.

AI's exponential concentration of wealth creates conditions identical to:

- late-stage Rome
- Qing Dynasty collapse
- French Ancien Régime
- pre-revolution Russia
- pre-reform China

History is repeating at digital speed.

4.9 The Hidden Mechanism: Why AI Concentration Accelerates Exponentially

AI accelerates inequality through a four-step feedback loop:

Step 1 — The wealthy buy compute.

Compute + data = intelligence.

Step 2 — AI replaces labor.

Labor demand falls → wages fall.

Step 3 — Profits rise.

Owners earn more → workers earn less.

Step 4 — Profits buy more AI.

AI → more automation → more profit → more AI.

This loop repeats — faster each time.

It is the economic equivalent of a runaway reaction.

The middle class is crushed between:

- falling wages
- rising prices
- rising rents
- rising healthcare costs
- rising asset inequality
- rising corporate power

The old mechanisms that once lifted workers — education, unions, mobility — have no effect in this new loop.

4.10 Why Capitalism Cannot Self-Correct

Traditional capitalism self-corrected through:

- wage competition
- talent shortages
- labor mobility
- unionization
- education
- market forces
- creative destruction

AI breaks every self-correction mechanism:

1. Wage competition disappears

AI does not ask for raises.

2. Talent shortages disappear

AI is infinite talent.

3. Labor mobility disappears

Jobs disappear.

4. Unionization becomes irrelevant

AI cannot be unionized.

5. Education becomes obsolete

AI learns faster than humans.

6. Market forces collapse

Monopolies dominate through data and computing.

7. Creative destruction stops

You cannot "disrupt" a trillion-parameter model trained on the world.

Capitalism loses its self-healing capacity.

Collapse becomes inevitable unless replaced with a new structure.

4.11 The Moral Crisis: What Happens to a Society With No Middle Class?

The middle class provides:

- dignity
- hope
- mobility
- stability
- shared norms
- societal glue

Without it, society becomes:

- angry

- anxious
- polarized
- violent
- unstable
- fragmented

People lose meaning when:

- work disappears
- identity disappears
- economic security disappears
- pride disappears
- purpose disappears

A post-middle-class society is not just poor —
it is lost.

People who lose economic stability do not become "free."
They become vulnerable.

They become targets for:

- extremists
- autocrats
- demagogues
- conspiracy movements
- digital cults

Economic collapse always triggers political collapse.

AI accelerates both.

4.12 The Middle Class Cannot Return Without Structural Redistribution

Politicians love promising:

- "We will bring back the middle class."
- "We will restore good jobs."
- "We will revive manufacturing."
- "We will protect workers."
- "We will rebuild the American Dream."

These promises are not just unrealistic —
they are structurally impossible under current economic rules.

To rebuild the middle class, you must rebuild:

- wage bargaining power
- labor scarcity
- employer dependence on workers
- job mobility
- broad economic participation

AI eliminates all five.

Even if:

- you raise minimum wage
- you subsidize training
- you invest in education
- you offer tax credits to employers
- you create incentives for hiring

the underlying math stays the same:

AI is cheaper, faster, more reliable, more scalable, and infinitely replicable.

Employers will always choose the option that:

- works 24 hours
- never complains
- never sleeps
- never asks for healthcare
- never organizes a union
- never resigns
- never negotiates
- never sues you
- never demands safety regulations

This is not "evil capitalism."
This is basic economic logic applied to non-human labor.

The middle class cannot return unless society restructures the entire system around guaranteed income, public services, and redistribution of AI-generated wealth.

4.13 The Rise of AI Aristocracy: A Cognitive Feudalism

AI creates a new class structure never seen in history:

1. The Cognitive Aristocrats (Top 0.01%)

The tiny group who own and control:

- foundational models
- national AI compute clusters
- proprietary datasets
- capital-intensive training pipelines
- global distribution networks

Their wealth multiplies faster than anyone can conceptualize.

2. The AI-Enabled Professionals (Top 10–15%)

Those who can use AI to amplify their productivity:

- senior engineers
- entrepreneurs with capital
- investors
- top-level consultants
- executives using AI-augmented decision systems

This group thrives **briefly but eventually shrinks as AI absorbs more of their roles.**

3. The AI-Dependent Majority (60–70%)

People who rely on:

- gig income
- unstable work
- part-time services
- small intermittent tasks
- AI-assigned microjobs
- state welfare to survive

This class lacks bargaining power, stability, and identity.

4. The Economically Excluded (10–20%)

People who fall out of the system entirely due to:

- lack of digital access
- lack of education
- age
- health issues
- geography
- political marginalization

This structure mirrors the late feudal era —
with tech giants replacing landowners.

Even traditional Marxist frameworks cannot fully describe this new arrangement,
because the key resource is no longer land or industrial capital —
it is intelligence itself.

When intelligence becomes a private asset,
feudalism becomes digital.

4.14 Why AI Aristocracy Is More Powerful Than Any Previous Elite

AI aristocracy has qualities that no previous ruling class possessed:

1. Scalability of Power

A king cannot be in two places at once.
An AI model can govern billions simultaneously.

2. Depth of Insight

No government, corporation, or empire ever had full behavioral data of entire populations.
AI aristocrats do.

3. Predictive Control

Empires reacted to events.
AI predicts events before they happen.

4. Economic Dominance

No aristocracy has ever controlled:

- every industry
- every job
- every skill
- every decision system
- every creative process

AI aristocrats will.

5. Political Influence

If AI becomes essential to national stability,
the corporations that own AI become more important than governments.

6. Cultural Control

AI models generate:

- news
- entertainment
- education
- advertising
- political messaging
- daily communication

They shape the "information environment" in ways no church, empire, or monarchy ever could.

The middle class does not simply disappear —
it is replaced by a new system where economic agency no longer exists for most people.

4.15 Why Redistribution Is Not a Choice — It Is the Only Stability Mechanism

Redistribution is not ideology.
It is engineering.
It is balancing forces that would otherwise tear society apart.

Without redistribution, you get:

- mass unemployment
- collapsing consumer demand
- falling birth rates
- extreme inequality
- crime waves
- political instability
- authoritarian government
- social fragmentation
- oligarchic control
- civil conflict

Redistribution becomes a pressure valve,
preventing the system from exploding under its own contradictions.

But redistribution must evolve to match the scale of AI-generated wealth.
This means:

1. Progressive Taxation up to 80%

AI owners accumulate wealth faster than any tax base in human history.
Without high taxation, inequality becomes uncontainable.

2. Universal Basic Income

Replaces wages as the foundation of consumption.

3. Universal Basic Services

Free healthcare, education, housing, transport, childcare, internet —
the pillars of human dignity.

4. AI Dividends

A share of the profits generated by national AI models paid to every citizen.

5. Public Ownership of Core AI Infrastructure

Not all AI must be state-owned, but the foundational models must be:

- transparent
- regulated

- democratically controlled

6. Wealth Smoothing Mechanisms

Policies preventing the formation of trillionaire dynasties.

Without these measures, society becomes ungovernable.

4.16 The Economic Shift: From Work-Based Identity to Human-Based Identity

The middle class identity of the 20th century was built on:

- job
- skill
- career
- profession
- expertise
- social status
- salary
- homeownership

This identity collapses in the AI age because:

- jobs disappear
- skills become automated
- careers evaporate
- professions shrink to near-zero
- expertise is absorbed by models
- salaries decline
- homeownership becomes unaffordable

A society that links identity to labor collapses psychologically when labor disappears.

A new identity must emerge — a post-work identity:

- community
- creativity
- learning
- contribution
- ethics
- caregiving

- human connection
- personal meaning
- self-realization
- civic participation
- cultural exploration

This shift is profound, and redistribution makes it possible.

People cannot find meaning if they are struggling to survive.

Redistribution is not merely economic —
it is existential.

4.17 Why the Middle Class Cannot Be Saved — But Humanity Can

The middle class as we know it is gone.

It will not be:

- restored
- revived
- recovered
- rebuilt
- protected
- maintained

It is not returning because the economic logic that created it has died.

But something better than the middle class can be built:

A society where:

- everything essential is guaranteed
- economic security is universal
- AI wealth is shared
- social mobility is redefined
- meaning is no longer linked to wage labor
- humans are free to pursue purpose, not survival

This is not the collapse of society.
This is the collapse of a very specific economic structure.

What comes next can be the most humane civilization ever created —
if we choose it.

4.18 Closing: The Great Redistribution of Intelligence

History has seen three great redistributions:

1. The redistribution of land (end of feudalism)
2. The redistribution of capital (rise of the middle class)
3. The redistribution of knowledge (the internet)

But now we stand on the edge of the greatest redistribution of all:

The redistribution of intelligence.

If intelligence is privatized,
we enter a new dark age.

If intelligence is shared,
we enter a new enlightenment.

The middle class dies in one scenario.
Humanity thrives in the other.

This is the real choice of the 21st century.

Capitalism cannot solve it.
Tax cuts cannot solve it.
Markets cannot solve it.
Old ideology cannot solve it.

It requires:

- new taxation
- new distribution
- new governance
- new social contracts
- new identity structures
- new purpose
- new values

A world where intelligence belongs to everyone

is a world where
no one is left behind.

This is the world the Utopia Humanity Society seeks to build.

4.19 How AI Reshapes Global Power: Why Nations Without Redistribution Will Collapse

The arrival of AI does not simply transform workplaces — it transforms geopolitics.
Every nation faces a new existential question:

"Can a country survive when 60–80% of its population has no economic role?"

Nations that fail to answer will experience:

- mass unemployment
- social unrest
- declining birth rates
- weakened national security
- brain drain
- collapse of consumer markets
- political extremism
- fragmentation of institutions

This will not be evenly distributed.
The countries that fall first will be those whose political ideologies prevent redistribution.

Low-tax nations lose fastest.

High-tax nations stabilize fastest.

AI increases national inequality far more dramatically than internal inequality.
The nations that:

- own compute
- own models
- own data
- redistribute benefits
- stabilize their populations
- ensure fairness

will become the superpowers of the AI age.

Power will no longer depend on military forces alone —

but on who can govern intelligence fairly.

Nations that continue to cling to neoliberal tax-cut ideology will disintegrate from internal contradictions before their AI systems even mature.

This means:

- The U.S. cannot survive long-term with low tax + high automation.
- The U.K. cannot survive long-term with austerity + AI labor collapse.
- Developing nations cannot rely on cheap labor because AI erases that advantage.

AI does not just disrupt companies —
it disrupts entire countries.

4.20 The End of the American Dream and the Chinese Dream

Two dominant national narratives have shaped the global imagination:

The American Dream:

"If you work hard, you can rise."

The Chinese Dream:

"If the nation grows, all people will prosper."

AI breaks both completely.

4.20.1 The American Dream Disintegrates

The American Dream depended on:

- wage growth
- job mobility
- entrepreneurial possibility

- strong middle class
- affordable education
- rising productivity
- meritocracy

AI destroys all seven.

With AI:

- wage growth stops
- job mobility disappears (jobs disappear entirely)
- entrepreneurial opportunity shrinks (compute monopolies dominate)
- middle class collapses
- education becomes irrelevant for employment
- productivity no longer raises wages
- meritocracy becomes impossible

Hard work stops translating into prosperity when machines outperform everyone.

The American Dream becomes mathematically impossible —
unless America redefines prosperity as a collective right, not an individual gamble.

4.20.2 The Chinese Dream Disintegrates

The Chinese Dream depended on:

- industrial labor
- infrastructure expansion
- export-led growth
- property market stability
- manufacturing dominance
- social mobility through education

AI destroys all six.

AI-driven manufacturing:

- ends China's labor advantage
- reverses outsourcing
- accelerates reshoring to the U.S. and Europe

- undercuts factories
- shrinks exports
- deflates land values
- obsoletes rote education

China's old model becomes unusable.
AI demands transparency, decentralization, and democratic accountability —
none of which align with CCP authoritarianism.

China faces a deeper crisis than the U.S., because:

- the state depends on employment to maintain loyalty
- the middle class depends on property values
- the economy depends on exports
- the political system depends on control

AI breaks all three pillars simultaneously.

The Chinese Dream becomes internally contradictory —
unless China embraces redistribution, autonomy, and citizen rights.

4.21 Why Authoritarian Capitalism Cannot Survive AI Either

Many believe that authoritarian systems will handle AI better because:

- they can force adoption
- they can centralize control
- they can coordinate resources
- they can regulate markets aggressively

This is a dangerous misconception.

Authoritarian capitalism cannot survive AI because:

1. AI exposes corruption.

Corrupt officials cannot hide inefficiency from AI auditing systems.

2. AI requires decentralized innovation.

Central planning cannot match the speed of open knowledge creation.

3. AI demands social trust.

Authoritarianism destroys trust; AI-driven transitions require it.

4. AI eliminates low-skill jobs.

Authoritarian regimes depend on keeping their populations employed for stability.

5. AI accelerates political awareness.

Information models reveal injustice and inequality instantly.

6. AI reduces the need for human administrators.

This undermines the bureaucratic base that authoritarian states rely on.

7. AI punishes secrecy.

Closed systems produce weaker models; open democracies produce stronger ones.

8. AI empowers citizens.

Knowledge is power — more accessible knowledge weakens autocracy.

In short:

Authoritarian capitalism cannot adapt fast enough to survive the transparency and efficiency of AI.

Those regimes that do not democratize will collapse.
Those that redistribute and decentralize will survive.

4.22 Designing a New Class Structure: The Four-Level Utopia Humanity Model

The question is not whether the middle class will disappear —
it will.

The real question is:

What replaces it?

The Utopia Humanity Society proposes a new four-level class architecture based on *dignity, not labor.*

Level 1: Universal Citizen Tier (Base Income + Services)

Every human receives:

- UBI
- free healthcare
- free education
- free housing access
- free transportation
- free digital infrastructure
- free AI tools
- free retraining
- free legal support

This tier eliminates poverty entirely.
It creates a floor of dignity.

Level 2: Contribution Tier (Voluntary Work + Creative Output)

People who choose to contribute receive:
- additional income
- social recognition
- project-based rewards
- opportunities for leadership
- community-building influence

Contribution becomes voluntary, not forced by survival.

Level 3: Innovation Tier (Entrepreneurs + Researchers + Creators)

Supported by:

- public AI infrastructure
- grants
- open-source models
- universal compute credits
- collaborative global networks

Anyone can innovate without needing capital.
Creativity becomes democratized.

Level 4: Stewardship Tier (AI Governance + Public Oversight)

This tier includes:

- elected AI auditors
- ethical boards
- citizen committees
- transparent model governance councils

The highest class is not the wealthy —
it is those entrusted with protecting the system.

This structure ends feudal concentration and replaces it with shared guardianship.

4.23 Final Synthesis: The Post-Capitalist Society of Shared Intelligence

The death of the middle class is not the end of society.
It is the end of an era.

Humanity stands at a crossroads:

Path 1 — Collapse

AI aristocracy

- unregulated monopolies
- low taxes
- dismantled welfare
- disappearing labor
- broken social trust
- authoritarian drift

= a global dark age

Path 2 — Transformation

High taxation

- shared AI ownership
- universal public goods
- UBI
- ethical AI governance
- new purpose for human life

= a new civilization

AI does not automatically liberate humanity.
AI only creates the possibility of liberation.

What determines the outcome is not the technology —
but the system we build around it.

The old world was built on:

- labor
- scarcity
- competition
- survival
- fear

The new world can be built on:

- dignity
- abundance
- creativity
- community
- freedom

Capitalism does not die because of ideology.
It dies because intelligence has been automated.

The Utopia Humanity Society is not a dream —
it is the only structurally coherent model for an AI-driven civilization.

We are not witnessing the end of wealth.
We are witnessing the end of *concentrated* wealth.

We are not witnessing the end of work.
We are witnessing the beginning of *human purpose beyond work*.

We are not witnessing the end of the middle class.
We are witnessing the birth of a world where classes lose meaning entirely.

This is not collapse.
This is transition.

This is not chaos.
This is evolution.

This is not the end.
This is the moment humanity becomes free.

4.24 Why the Collapse of the Middle Class Is Not a Failure — It Is a Signal

Every major societal transformation announces itself not with words,
but with pain.

The death of the middle class is not an economic accident.
It is a signal —
a warning flare telling humanity that the system which carried us through the
19th and 20th centuries has reached its limits.

The middle class emerged from the industrial revolution.
It disappears in the intelligence revolution.

In the same way that:

- the hunter-gatherer world was replaced by agriculture
- agriculture was replaced by industrialism
- industrialism is now replaced by automation

the middle class is disappearing because the world that needed it no longer
exists.

This is not failure.
This is evolution.

This is the moment to build something better.

4.25 The Psychological Collapse: When Work Can No Longer Define Human Worth

The death of the middle class forces a psychological transformation as profound as the economic one.

For 200 years, society has repeated a single message:

> "Your value comes from your job."

This idea shaped:

- education
- culture
- family expectations
- social status
- personal identity
- political rhetoric
- the entire moral structure of capitalism

But AI breaks this belief completely.

When a model can:

- write legal briefs
- draft medical diagnoses
- create business plans
- design products
- compose music
- manage operations
- negotiate contracts
- predict market behavior
- tutor children
- create art
- do scientific reasoning
- write code
- fix code
- generate entire startups

then work no longer defines human worth.

Humans are forced into a new frontier:

If work disappears, who are you?

If jobs end, what is your purpose?
If careers dissolve, where do you find meaning?

The answer becomes clearer in the Utopia Humanity Society:

Meaning is no longer earned — it is lived.
Purpose is no longer assigned — it is chosen.
Identity is no longer economic — it is human.

4.26 AI Makes Everyone Rich in Theory — But Everyone Poor in Practice (Unless Redistribution Exists)

AI has the potential to create infinite wealth.

AI-driven manufacturing and services can bring marginal cost to:

- almost zero
- forever
- globally

In theory, this makes society rich.

But in practice, without redistribution, AI makes:

- the AI owners infinitely wealthy
- everyone else infinitely dependent

Why?

Because AI collapses labor value, and without labor value:

- wages fall
- income concentrates
- demand collapses
- the economy destabilizes

AI abundance becomes poverty for the majority because:

Abundance without distribution destroys social systems.

Abundance with distribution creates utopia.

Capitalism is incapable of managing abundance.
Only democratic redistribution can.

This is not ideology —
it is system design.

4.27 The Final Choice:

Private Intelligence vs. Shared Intelligence

Humanity now stands at the most important decision in economic history.

Not free market vs. socialism.
Not capitalism vs. communism.
Not left vs. right.

Those are 20th-century battles.

The real choice is:

Option 1 — Private Intelligence (Collapse)

A world where intelligence belongs to:

- corporations
- billionaires
- authoritarian states
- private military forces
- monopolies
- hereditary dynasties

This world becomes:

- unstable
- unequal
- violent
- apathetic
- feudal
- hopeless

Human dignity dissolves.

Option 2 — Shared Intelligence (Civilization)

A world where intelligence is:

- publicly governed
- widely accessible
- equally beneficial
- ethically regulated
- distributed as a common resource

This world becomes:

- stable
- equal
- peaceful
- innovative
- cooperative
- prosperous

Human dignity expands.

Here is the truth:

AI is not only the end of capitalism —

it is the end of every system that concentrates power.

The only sustainable civilization is one that shares intelligence, not hoards it.

This includes:

- taxing the wealthy up to 80%
- distributing AI profits to all
- providing UBI
- guaranteeing public services
- regulating AI monopolies
- democratizing ethics and oversight
- ensuring every citizen has access to the tools of creation
- protecting digital rights as human rights

The collapse of the middle class is the final warning:
humanity must evolve or face instability, conflict, and decline.

4.28 Closing: The Birth of a Society Beyond Classes

The middle class disappears,
but something greater emerges:
a society where class itself loses meaning.

In the Utopia Humanity Society:

- wealth is shared
- intelligence is shared
- opportunities are shared
- dignity is universal
- freedom is guaranteed
- creativity is limitless
- survival is automatic
- purpose is chosen
- community is renewed
- humanity evolves

This is not utopia as fantasy.
This is utopia as engineering.

Capitalism produced wealth but could not distribute it.
Communism attempted distribution but failed to create wealth.
AI allows humanity to do both:

Infinite wealth + universal distribution = the next stage of civilization.

The death of the middle class is not the end.
It is the beginning.

The world that comes next is not defined by jobs, wages, or productivity.
It is defined by shared intelligence, shared prosperity, and shared humanity.

This is the future the Utopia Humanity Society chooses.

And this is the future humanity deserves.

CHAPTER 5: WHY AUTHORITARIAN SYSTEMS CANNOT MANAGE AI

How Closed Political Structures Collapse Under Open Technologies

Authoritarian regimes claim they can manage anything.
They promise stability, order, efficiency, discipline, "social harmony," and the ability to "plan the future" with the precision of an engineer.

For decades they believed — and convinced millions — that:

- controlling information ensures unity
- controlling citizens ensures stability
- controlling markets ensures progress
- controlling dissent ensures loyalty
- controlling narratives ensures legitimacy

But in the age of AI, this logic collapses.

Artificial intelligence is not merely a tool.
It is a new form of *collective cognition* —
a system that requires transparency, open data, error correction, distributed participation, and a free flow of information.

These conditions are the opposite of authoritarianism.

Authoritarianism survives only when:

- information is restricted
- criticism is censored
- power is centralized
- truth is monopolized
- dissent is punished
- fear regulates behavior

AI survives only when:

- information flows freely
- errors are openly exposed
- systems are audited
- data is shared
- feedback is encouraged

- transparency is maintained

The two systems cannot coexist.

why every authoritarian state — no matter its power, size, or ideology — will fail to deploy AI safely, effectively, or sustainably.

AI is the acid that dissolves dictatorship,
because dictatorship is built on secrecy,
and AI is built on transparency.

5.1 Authoritarianism Requires Control — AI Requires Openness

At its core, authoritarianism is a system of information control.

Totalitarian states do not fear bombs.
They fear facts.

They fear:

- accurate statistics
- independent journalism
- transparency reports
- whistleblowers
- audits
- free speech
- independent courts
- academic research
- historical truth

Because truth is destabilizing to a system built on propaganda.

But AI cannot function without truth.

AI must be trained on real data.

AI must be allowed to correct itself.
AI must expose mistakes.
AI must surface contradictions.
AI must improve through feedback.

In authoritarian systems:

- data is falsified
- statistics are inflated
- corruption is hidden
- failures are censored
- problems are politically sensitive
- truth is dangerous
- transparency is punished
- feedback is suppressed
- criticism is criminalized

A system that hides reality cannot manage a technology that depends on it.

This is the first and deepest contradiction.

5.2 AI Exposes Corruption, Incompetence, and Lies — Making Authoritarian Stability Impossible

Authoritarian systems survive through carefully curated illusion:

- "everything is stable"
- "the economy is strong"
- "the leaders are wise"
- "everyone supports the party"
- "there are no internal conflicts"
- "we have no social problems"
- "critics are foreign agents"

AI destroys these illusions by automatically detecting and surfacing:

- inconsistencies in official data
- fraudulent financial reports
- ghost projects
- nepotism networks
- propaganda patterns
- censorship gaps
- regional policy failures
- supply chain manipulation
- shadow corruption groups

An authoritarian state cannot allow this truth to be visible —

not even internally.

Because once AI reveals the scale of:
- corruption
- incompetence
- abuse
- mismanagement
- inequality
- social mistrust

the regime's legitimacy collapses.

Authoritarians cannot tolerate truth,
and AI cannot function without truth.

Therefore:

Authoritarian AI must be crippled —

by design —
to avoid revealing the system's own defects.

And crippled AI is obsolete AI.
They cannot compete.

5.3 AI Requires Decentralized Innovation — Authoritarianism Requires Centralized Power

Modern AI advances because:

- thousands of independent researchers collaborate
- open-source models evolve rapidly
- academic communities share new methods
- global datasets are accessible
- companies iterate publicly
- feedback is global

Authoritarian states operate in the opposite direction:

- research must serve political goals
- sensitive topics are prohibited
- foreign collaboration is restricted

- academic freedom is impossible
- "politically incorrect" results are banned
- innovation funnels through the party

The result?

Authoritarian AI becomes slow, inaccurate, politicized, fragile, and ultimately useless.

Compare this with open societies:

- developers critique each other freely
- failures are documented publicly
- datasets are shared
- code is forked
- models are improved transparently
- global talent collaborates

Authoritarian states try to compete with:

- censorship
- coercion
- slogans
- propaganda
- "national AI champions"
- patriotic mobilization campaigns

But AI is not built by slogans.
It is built by truth and iteration.

You cannot order innovation through fear.

You cannot command creativity through obedience.

You cannot produce global intelligence through national isolation.

5.4 "Fake Communism" States Cannot Transition to Post-Labor AI Societies

Countries calling themselves "communist" are not communist.

They are state-capitalist authoritarian regimes with:
- capitalist inequality

- capitalist exploitation
- capitalist corruption
- capitalist class hierarchy

But without:

- free elections
- independent unions
- citizen rights
- transparency
- accountability
- redistribution mechanisms
- public oversight
- genuine democracy

They adopt the symbol of communism
but practice a system even more unequal than Western capitalism.

AI makes this contradiction unsustainable.

In a post-labor world:

- wealth must be redistributed
- AI dividends must be shared
- public services must be universal
- tax must be high on elites
- democracy must be real
- transparency must be mandatory
- power must be decentralized

Fake communist states cannot do any of this.

They cannot redistribute wealth because elites depend on inequality.
They cannot empower citizens because the system relies on obedience.
They cannot allow transparency because corruption is systemic.
They cannot democratize intelligence because citizens are viewed as threats.

This means:

Authoritarian states cannot transition into the Utopia Humanity Society.

They will collapse under their own contradictions.

5.5 Surveillance States Misunderstand AI's Nature

Authoritarians believe AI is a surveillance tool,
a weapon for:

- monitoring citizens
- predicting dissent
- enforcing loyalty
- controlling behavior
- manipulating public opinion
- strengthening power

But this is a fundamental misunderstanding of AI's long-term nature.

Yes, AI can temporarily increase authoritarian control.
But in the long run:

AI makes centralized control impossible.

Here's why:

1. AI increases the volume of data beyond what the state can filter.

Too much truth leaks.

2. AI empowers individual citizens with intelligence.

Even censored models reveal contradictions.

3. AI accelerates communication.

People can coordinate faster than censorship.

4. AI enables anonymous truth-sharing.

Models can generate explanations of injustice in coded ways.

5. AI reveals the inefficiency of authoritarian governance.

The system cannot hide its incompetence.

Surveillance states imagine AI as a cage.

But AI is a solvent —
it dissolves the bars, slowly and silently.

5.6 Closed Systems Cannot Compete With Open Systems

Every major technological era proves the same pattern:

- open societies innovate faster
- open debate produces stronger ideas
- open data reveals errors early
- open collaboration accelerates breakthroughs
- open criticism improves quality
- open institutions attract global talent

Closed systems, no matter how wealthy or disciplined, fall behind.

The Soviet Union could build rockets
but could not build personal computers.

China can build factories
but cannot build the foundational AI architecture needed to lead the world.

Authoritarian systems can:

- copy
- steal
- reverse engineer

But they cannot:

- innovate
- collaborate globally
- create new paradigms
- attract world-leading talent
- admit mistakes
- self-correct
- allow disruptive thinkers
- tolerate intellectual independence

AI punishes systems that cannot self-correct.

And authoritarianism is, by definition,

a system that cannot self-correct.

5.7 Democracy as the Only Stable Model for AI Governance

There is a profound misunderstanding in the world today.

Many assume:

- Authoritarian regimes are efficient.
- Democracies are slow.
- Technocracy outperforms politics.
- Centralized states can "command" AI.

But this is the opposite of true.

AI does not reward efficiency.
AI rewards transparency, correction, diversity, openness, adaptability, and accountability —
all characteristics of democratic systems.

Here is why democracy is the only structure capable of managing AI.

5.7.1 AI Depends on Error Correction — Democracy Is a System Built on Correction

Authoritarian regimes suppress negative feedback:

- Failed policies cannot be criticized.
- Leaders cannot be challenged.
- Data cannot be corrected.
- Experts cannot speak openly.
- Whistleblowers are punished.
- Journalists are censored.

This creates a *politically convenient version of reality*,
which is useless for AI.

Democracy, by contrast, is built on:

- criticism
- opposition
- transparency

- investigative journalism
- accountability
- public scrutiny
- free debate
- open data
- competing perspectives

Democracy has evolved for centuries as a giant error-correction machine.

AI is also an error-correction machine.

Authoritarianism is a truth-suppression machine.

Only one of these can coexist with AI.

5.7.2 AI Requires Distributed Innovation — Democracy Liberates Talent

AI breakthroughs emerge when:

- researchers challenge assumptions
- outsiders contribute new ideas
- community members build open-source models
- individuals experiment without permission
- companies compete freely
- criticisms are openly published
- academic freedom flourishes

Authoritarian regimes cannot allow any of this.

Innovation requires:

- psychological safety
- freedom from political punishment
- intellectual exploration
- collaborative ecosystems
- global participation

When fear enters the equation,
innovation dies.

This is why authoritarian AI development slows down:

- talented researchers leave
- ambitious thinkers self-censor
- the smartest minds hide their ideas
- the entire system becomes risk-averse

Democracy, by contrast, produces:
- bold experiments
- open-source breakthroughs
- collective intelligence
- global collaboration
- honest peer review
- free criticism
- strong institutions

This is why the leading AI companies are in democratic nations.

It is not an accident.
It is structural.

5.7.3 AI Requires Algorithmic Transparency — Democracy Demands Accountability

AI systems must be:

- explainable
- auditable
- debuggable
- reviewable
- legally accountable

Authoritarian regimes cannot do this, because:

- transparency exposes corruption
- audits reveal mismanagement
- accountability weakens power
- transparency threatens legitimacy

Democracy requires transparency as a survival condition.

AI requires transparency as a functional condition.

This alignment makes democracy the only durable model for AI governance.

5.7.4 AI Amplifies the Dangers of Power Concentration — Democracies Distribute Power

AI gives enormous power to whoever controls:

- compute
- models
- data
- surveillance systems
- infrastructure
- institutions

If this power is concentrated in:

- one leader
- one party
- one elite group
- one security agency

then society collapses into computational authoritarianism.

Democracy — with separation of powers, judicial independence, civil liberties, and pluralism — is the only system capable of ensuring:

- distributed oversight
- checks and balances
- public involvement
- legal accountability
- ethical governance

Authoritarianism has none of these.

AI in an authoritarian system becomes a weapon.
AI in a democratic system becomes a tool.

Only one is sustainable.

5.8 Case Studies: Why Closed Political Systems Cannot Manage AI

Let us examine concrete examples:
China, Russia, and Iran — three major authoritarian states pursuing AI development.

Each faces the same systemic contradictions.
Each reveals a different aspect of authoritarian failure.

5.8.1 China — The Paradox of Total Data and Zero Truth

China has:

- massive datasets
- strong engineering talent
- huge compute clusters
- centralized government planning
- national AI strategies

From the outside, it looks unstoppable.

But China faces the deepest contradiction:

It has unlimited data —

but cannot allow real data.

Because:

- officials falsify numbers
- local governments hide failures
- companies inflate performance
- pandemic reporting is censored
- poverty statistics are manipulated
- corruption is buried
- criticism is forbidden

AI trained on politically manipulated data becomes:

- inaccurate
- biased
- fragile

- untrustworthy

Moreover:

AI cannot expose corruption in China

because exposing corruption threatens political power.

So all meaningful AI applications (audits, transparency, risk detection, public health analytics) are deliberately crippled.

China can build AI hardware.
China can build surveillance AI.
But China cannot build self-correcting AI.

Because self-correction requires truth.

And truth is forbidden.

5.8.2 Russia — AI in a State That Cannot Modernize

Russia faces a different contradiction.

Russia has:

- strong mathematicians
- cybersecurity experts
- military AI researchers

But it lacks:
- industrial capacity
- competitive markets
- independent institutions
- open academic collaboration
- investment capital
- political stability

AI cannot flourish in a state:

- without global participation
- without economic dynamism
- without institutional trust

- without private sector competition
- without a stable legal system

Russia attempts to build AI as a military tool.

But this produces only:
- weaponized misinformation
- surveillance systems
- cyber operations

These are not the foundations of AI leadership.
They are the foundations of geopolitical stagnation.

Russia cannot transition to a post-labor society because:
- wealth is extracted, not created
- elites resist redistribution
- corruption is systemic
- institutions are hollow
- the social contract is broken

AI cannot fix a collapsing state.
AI accelerates the collapse.

5.8.3 Iran — The Limits of Ideological Control

Iran has:

- educated youth
- strong diaspora talent
- innovative thinkers

But the state is built on:

- ideological censorship
- digital repression
- religious dogma
- political paranoia

AI cannot function in a society where:

- history is rewritten
- science is censored
- dissent is illegal

- internet is restricted
- datasets are tightly controlled

Iran's brightest engineers leave.
Its institutions lose legitimacy.
Its society becomes disconnected from global innovation.

AI thrives on openness.
But Iran survives on closure.

Iran cannot create or manage AI systems that require:

- global data
- open-source collaboration
- transparent models
- shared intelligence

Authoritarianism suffocates talent,
and without talent, AI dies.

5.9 Why Control-Based Societies Collapse in the Age of AI

Authoritarian states are built on:

- hierarchy
- fear
- secrecy
- propaganda
- obedience

AI undermines each pillar.

5.9.1 AI Destroys Hierarchy

AI makes experts obsolete.
This threatens authoritarian elites who depend on hierarchy for legitimacy.

5.9.2 AI Destroys Fear-Based Control

If citizens have AI assistants:

- censorship becomes harder
- propaganda becomes obvious
- truth becomes easier to discover
- coordination becomes easier

Fear loses power.

5.9.3 AI Destroys Secrecy

AI reveals:

- corruption
- inefficiency
- manipulation
- failures
- incompetence

Secrecy becomes impossible.

5.9.4 AI Destroys Propaganda

AI models can:

- detect manipulation
- debunk narratives
- expose logical contradictions
- spread counter-information anonymously

Propaganda ecosystems collapse.

5.9.5 AI Destroys Obedience

AI empowers:

- curiosity
- knowledge
- communication

- coordination
- analysis
- intelligence

Obedience is replaced by understanding.

Understanding is the enemy of authoritarianism.

5.10 Closing:

AI Does Not Strengthen Dictatorships — AI Ends Them

There is a myth spreading in the world:

> "AI will help dictators control society."

> This is only partially true.
> AI can give dictators temporary tools:

- surveillance
- censorship
- social credit systems
- propaganda generation

But these tools have short-term benefits and long-term fatal consequences.

Because AI requires:

- truth
- transparency
- open criticism
- distributed innovation
- accurate data
- participatory governance
- accountability

All of these destroy authoritarian logic.

Authoritarian regimes believe:

"If we control AI, we control society."

But the reality is:

If they try to control AI, they destroy their ability to use it.
If they try to use AI, they destroy their ability to control society.

This contradiction cannot be resolved.

AI is the beginning of the end of:

- secrecy
- propaganda
- censorship
- rigid hierarchy
- political control
- authoritarian ideology

AI does not strengthen dictatorship.
AI exposes it, accelerates its contradictions, and ultimately collapses it.

The only societies that can survive the AI future are:

- democratic
- transparent
- accountable
- redistributive
- participatory
- open
- humane
- rights-based

This is why the Utopia Humanity Society is not merely a political preference —
it is the only viable civilization model in the age of AI.

And authoritarianism,
no matter how powerful it looks today,
is already in its final chapter.

CHAPTER 6: THE LIE OF "COMMUNISM" UNDER ONE-PARTY STATES

Why One-Party Regimes Are Not Communist, Not Socialist —

But Neo-Feudal Aristocracies Incompatible with an AI-Driven Humane Society

For decades, regimes such as China, North Korea, Vietnam, Cuba, and the former Soviet Union have claimed the mantle of *communism* — using the word to justify:
- one-party rule
- suppression of dissent
- state control of media
- elimination of political competition
- overwhelming central authority
- economic planning monopolized by a small elite

To the outside world, this branding produces confusion.
To their own citizens, it produces fear, resignation, and fatalism.

People are told:

"This is communism."
"You have no choice."
"The Party decides your future."
"The system exists for the people — even if the people disagree."

But this is not a misunderstanding.
It is a **strategic, calculated, historically engineered lie**.

These regimes are not communist.
They never were.
They never will be.

They are **not socialist**,
not even distorted versions of capitalism.

They are something older — and far more dangerous:

Neo-Feudal Aristocracies disguised in communist language.

Here is :

why the label of "communism" was chosen as camouflage,

why **neo-feudal systems cannot survive the AI era**,

let alone transition into a humane, post-labor civilization.

6.1 Communism as an Ideal vs. Neo-Feudal Reality

To understand the deception, we must separate two radically different things:

Communism as a philosophical ideal

vs.

"Communism" as practiced by one-party authoritarian states

Communism (as theory) is based on:
- public ownership of the means of production
- abolition of economic classes
- equality regardless of background
- democratic worker governance
- elimination of exploitative hierarchies
- transparency in collective decision-making
- human-centered economic distribution

One-party "communist" states are based on:
- party ownership of production
- creation of a hereditary political elite
- political hierarchy replacing economic hierarchy
- loyalty replacing competence
- suppression of worker autonomy
- opacity, secrecy, and fear
- centralized control without accountability
- elite accumulation of wealth
- surveillance as governance

These two systems share **nothing** in common.

One seeks to liberate human beings.
The other seeks to **manage, rank, and discipline them**.

One requires democracy.
The other eliminates it.

Therefore:

> **All one-party "communist" regimes are fake communism.**
> **They are not left-wing.**
> **They are not socialist.**
> **They are neo-feudal aristocracies painted red.**

> Understanding this structural reality is essential
> before explaining why these systems collapse under AI.

6.2 The Political Economy of Neo-Feudal Aristocracy

What actually exists in these regimes is not socialism,
but a **modern revival of feudal power relations**.

6.2.1 Who Owns the Means of Production?

Official narrative:
"The people own the factories."

Structural reality:
Ownership is concentrated in:

- party families
- state-controlled conglomerates
- military-industrial networks
- politically protected monopolies

These entities function as:

- rent-extraction machines
- monopolistic empires
- patronage systems
- political-economic clans

Ordinary citizens have:

- no ownership rights
- no dividends
- no transparency
- no decision-making power

This is not communism.

It is **a political aristocracy** —
a modern form of feudal lordship.

6.2.2 Who Controls Information?

Real communism requires shared information
to empower workers and communities.

Neo-feudal regimes require **information monopoly**
to protect hierarchy.

This includes:

- censorship
- propaganda
- banned topics
- falsified statistics
- rewritten history

Communism cannot survive without truth.
Neo-feudal power cannot survive **with** truth.

6.2.3 Who Benefits from Economic Growth?

In genuine egalitarian systems, growth is distributed.

In neo-feudal systems, growth is **captured** by:

- ruling families
- party-business alliances
- military elites
- politically loyal networks

Despite socialist branding, inequality in China today exceeds that of many capitalist democracies.

This is not socialism.
It is **feudal rent extraction enforced by modern state power**.

6.2.4 Who Makes Decisions?

Communist theory envisions:

- worker councils
- collective deliberation
- democratic assemblies

Neo-feudal reality delivers:

- one party
- one leadership core
- zero elections
- zero accountability
- zero checks and balances
- decisions made in sealed rooms

This is **monarchy dressed as Marxism**.

These regimes are **neither socialist nor capitalist variants**.
They represent a structural regression:

Neo-Feudal Aristocracy

where:

- power is allocated like fiefdoms
- resources are inherited like titles
- loyalty outweighs ability
- obedience is safer than creativity
- law serves hierarchy, not justice

Medieval feudalism ruled by blood and land.
Modern neo-feudalism rules by party, ideology, and coercive institutions.

This structure — not ideology — is why such systems cannot coexist with AI.

6.3 The Origins of the Lie: Why "Communism" Was Chosen as a Cover

Neo-Feudal Aristocratic regimes did not choose communism by accident.

It was a deliberate, strategically engineered, historically constructed decision—because *communism*, as a word and a legacy, is uniquely suited to legitimizing extreme concentrations of feudal-style power under a modern disguise.

The label was chosen because it can be used to:

1 Legitimize the elimination of political opposition

"Opposition = bourgeois enemies of the people."

2 Legitimize total state control of media and information

"Propaganda = ideological education."

3 Legitimize the seizure of private property

"Confiscation = collectivization."

4 Legitimize permanent one-party rule

"Pluralism = capitalist infiltration."

5 Legitimize the suppression of dissent and free thought

"Criticism = counterrevolution."

Thus, *communism* becomes the perfect excuse:

"We are not neo-feudal rulers.
We are protecting the people's revolution."

This lie has been extraordinarily effective because:

- The West has long misunderstood the gap between communist theory and authoritarian practice
- Eastern societies fear the real-world consequences of opposing the ruling party
- The global left often romanticizes failed regimes
- The global right uses these regimes to attack social democracy
- Neo-feudal elites exploit communist language to conceal their aristocratic power structures

Fake communism is one of the most successful political branding strategies in modern history.

But AI will end it.

6.4 Why Fake Communism Cannot Survive the AI Revolution

AI fundamentally requires:

- transparency
- honest and accurate data
- distributed participation
- individual rights
- open communication
- public oversight
- democratic legitimacy

By contrast, communist-branded **neo-feudal aristocracies** depend on:

- secrecy
- falsified data
- extreme centralization
- censorship
- fear-based governance
- propaganda systems
- political loyalty over competence

These two systems are structurally incompatible.

AI is light.
Neo-feudal power is darkness.

Light does not negotiate with darkness.

It replaces it.

Let us examine the core contradictions.

6.4.1 Contradiction One:

AI Requires Truth — Neo-Feudal Aristocracy Requires Lies

A system built on propaganda cannot feed real data into AI.

If it does:

- corruption becomes visible
- incompetence becomes measurable
- wealth concentration becomes quantifiable
- inequality becomes undeniable
- human rights abuses become systematically exposed

No neo-feudal aristocracy can allow this.

Therefore:

AI under neo-feudal rule must be deliberately blinded.

But crippled AI cannot compete with democratic AI.

6.4.2 Contradiction Two:

AI Requires Rights — Neo-Feudal Aristocracy Eliminates Rights

In a post-labor society, the following become necessities:

- Universal Basic Income (UBI)
- universal healthcare
- free education
- social welfare systems
- progressive taxation
- democratic oversight

Neo-feudal aristocracies cannot allow:

- redistribution (it threatens elite privilege)
- transparency (it exposes corruption)
- participation (it creates political alternatives)
- independent welfare systems (they weaken dependence on the ruling hierarchy)

Thus:

Fake communism cannot build a stable AI-based welfare state.

It must choose between:

- protecting the aristocracy

or

- protecting society

It always chooses the aristocracy.

6.4.3 Contradiction Three:

AI Empowers Individuals — Neo-Feudal Aristocracy Depends on Subjugation

AI gives individuals:

- knowledge
- decision-making capacity
- analytical tools
- creative power
- access to global ideas
- the ability to question authority

Neo-feudal systems rely on:

- ignorance
- isolation
- obedience
- information monopolies
- ideological conditioning
- internalized fear

AI destroys this psychological architecture.

A citizen equipped with AI cannot remain a subject.

6.4.4 Contradiction Four:

AI Requires Innovation — Neo-Feudal Aristocracy Punishes Innovation

Innovation requires:

- debate
- risk-taking
- challenging authority
- unconventional thinking
- sharp criticism
- tolerance for failure

Neo-feudal aristocracies punish all of these as:

- dangerous
- subversive
- politically incorrect
- destabilizing

The result is inevitable:

- innovation collapses
- talent exits
- risk disappears
- fear dominates

Innovation stagnation is a fatal condition in the AI era.

6.5 Case Study: China — Neo-Feudal Aristocracy Behind Socialist Language

China is the most important example of fake communism, not because its rhetoric is loud, but because it combines:

- massive economic scale
- long-term socialist branding
- widespread Western misinterpretation
- internal contradictions amplified by AI

- the sharpest structural clash between **Neo-Feudal Aristocracy** and the AI era

To understand the deception, we must ignore slogans and examine the structure.

6.5.1 "Communism" as Political Branding

The Chinese state describes itself as:

- "socialism with Chinese characteristics"
- "the vanguard of communism"
- "the representative of the working class"
- "the people's government"

But structurally, China is not socialist.

It is a **modern Neo-Feudal Aristocracy**:
a hierarchical system where political loyalty, inherited access, and protected privilege determine power.

This is not ideology.
It is measurable reality:

- a large, politically connected billionaire class
- dominant monopolistic enterprises protected by power
- land and real estate used as political allocation tools
- systemic labor exploitation
- independent unions prohibited
- one of the world's highest inequality levels
- enforced rural-urban hierarchy
- public assets privatized through political networks
- data adjusted to political needs

Where is communism?
Where is socialism?
Where is worker ownership?

Only in slogans, propaganda, textbooks — and repression.

6.5.2 From Class Equality to Hereditary Privilege

Real communist ideals, at minimum, claim:

- abolition of class privilege
- worker ownership
- equal political rights
- democratic decision-making

China's reality is the inverse:

- the Party replaced the capitalist class
- political insiders replaced landlords
- elite families formed dynastic structures
- corruption became systemic
- loyalty replaced competence
- social mobility collapsed

A new ruling class emerged:

**Red aristocracy —
a modern feudal elite dressed in socialist language.**

Workers own nothing.
Citizens decide nothing.
The Party controls everything.

This is not communism.
It is **Neo-Feudal Aristocracy**.

6.5.3 The Social Contract: Silence for Growth

For four decades, China's social contract was simple:

- the regime delivers growth
- the population remains politically silent

This created surface stability, but conditional legitimacy:

- growth slows → legitimacy erodes
- unemployment rises → stability fractures
- middle class weakens → trust collapses

AI accelerates all three.

China's model relied on:

- cheap labor
- export manufacturing
- real estate inflation
- infrastructure expansion
- demographic advantage

AI dismantles each pillar:

- automation erases labor advantage
- repetitive jobs disappear
- analytical white-collar work is replaced
- property speculation loses relevance
- demographics no longer protect growth

Democracies absorb downturns.
Neo-feudal systems struggle to survive them.

6.5.4 AI Exposes Structural Contradictions

China faces an unsolvable paradox:

It needs AI to modernize,
but cannot allow AI to weaken political control.

Because:

- AI requires truthful data → the system relies on censorship
- AI requires error correction → the system punishes reporting problems
- AI requires openness → the system blocks information flow
- AI exposes falsified statistics → falsification is routine
- AI maps corruption → corruption sustains the hierarchy

To protect the regime, AI must be crippled.

But crippled AI cannot compete globally.

China's AI paradox is absolute:

Let AI function → power erodes
Restrict AI → the nation falls behind

There is no middle path.

6.5.5 Why China Cannot Enter a Post-Labor Society

The AI era requires:

- high taxation of extreme wealth
- redistribution
- universal basic income
- universal public services
- shared AI dividends
- transparency
- democratic oversight
- public ownership of intelligence

Neo-Feudal Aristocracy rejects every requirement:

- high taxes threaten privilege
- redistribution breaks power networks
- UBI removes dependence
- transparency exposes corruption
- oversight weakens one-party authority
- public intelligence dissolves monopoly

Without structural political reform, transition is impossible.

AI does not fit inside neo-feudal systems.
It dismantles them.

6.6 Why One-Party Systems Cannot Transition

One-party states are structurally frozen:

- no leadership rotation
- no correction mechanisms
- no peaceful transition
- no institutional competition
- no intellectual diversity

- no rights-based legitimacy

Post-labor societies require the opposite:

- adaptive institutions
- transparent governance
- citizen participation
- independent media
- checks and balances

The structures are incompatible.

6.7 AI as the Final Exposure of Fake Communism

Neo-feudal regimes survive through:

- myth
- slogans
- propaganda
- historical revision
- textbook control

AI dismantles these tools by:

- instantly detecting narrative contradictions
- enabling anonymous truth transmission
- revealing inequality and corruption automatically

A system built on concealment collapses when concealment fails.

6.8 Closing: Utopia Requires Democracy, Not Neo-Feudalism

One-party regimes monopolized the language of liberation while delivering:

- inequality
- repression
- elite capture
- censorship
- surveillance
- fear

They used emancipatory language to build systems of domination.

AI resets the equation.

The real choice is:

**Fake Communism
(Neo-Feudal Aristocracy + propaganda)**

or

**Humane Post-Labor Society
(democracy + rights + redistribution + transparency)**

The future does not belong to:

- one-party rule
- dictatorships
- pseudo-socialism
- censorship-based stability

The future belongs to societies that:

- distribute intelligence
- share wealth
- empower citizens
- protect rights
- prioritize dignity over authority

AI will not destroy neo-feudal systems overnight.
But it will weaken them irreversibly.

And that is the turning point of this century.

CHAPTER 7: THE NORDIC MODEL AS CIVILIZATION PROTOTYPE

Why the Post-Labor, AI-Driven Future Looks Most Like Denmark, Sweden, Norway, Finland, and Iceland

When people imagine the future, they often picture:

- skyscrapers of glass
- flying vehicles
- robots performing daily tasks
- AI assistants managing society
- fully automated factories
- self-regulating resource systems

But this is only the technological dimension of the future.
The real question is:

What social architecture is capable of absorbing AI,

managing abundance,
and distributing dignity?

The answer is not science fiction.
It already exists.

The Nordic countries — Denmark, Sweden, Norway, Finland, and Iceland — have quietly become the closest real-world blueprint for the post-capitalist civilization the AI era demands.

Not because they are perfect.
Not because they are utopian.
But because their core structure matches what the future requires:

- high taxes
- universal services
- redistributive economics
- transparency
- trust
- democratic accountability
- gender equality
- strong labor protections

- low inequality
- high innovation
- robust public institutions
- respect for human rights
- collaborative culture

These characteristics are not luxuries.
They are requirements for any society that wishes to survive and thrive in a world where:

- labor is no longer the foundation of the economy
- AI automates mental and physical work
- productivity is driven by machines, not humans
- wealth creation becomes detached from effort
- distribution becomes the central challenge

The Nordic model is the closest living prototype
of the Utopia Humanity Society
this book envisions.

This chapter explains why.

7.1 The Nordic Model: A Brief Overview of Its Structure

The Nordic model is built on six pillars:

1. High progressive taxation
2. Universal basic services (not income, but services)
3. Labor rights + strong union representation
4. Powerful public institutions
5. Low inequality + societal trust
6. Democratic accountability + transparency

Each pillar aligns perfectly with the needs of an AI-driven post-labor world.

Let us examine each one closely.

7.1.1 High Progressive Taxation — The Backbone of Civilizational Stability

Nordic countries tax:

- the rich
- corporations
- capital gains
- inheritance
- emissions
- luxury consumption

Tax rates on high-income earners can reach 55%–70%, depending on country and structure.

Critics scream:

"High tax kills growth!"
"High tax kills innovation!"
"High tax punishes success!"

But the data reveals the opposite:

- Nordic countries consistently score the highest in innovation indexes
- They have the world's healthiest startup ecosystems per capita
- Their public education systems produce highly capable workforces
- They maintain world-leading productivity
- They experience extremely high social mobility

High tax creates a stable base for innovation by ensuring:
- no one falls through the cracks
- failure is not catastrophic
- talent can take risks
- entrepreneurs are protected
- children start life with equal opportunity
- healthcare is guaranteed
- public trust is strong

This is the exact kind of environment needed for an AI-driven society where:

risk-taking and creativity matter far more than repetitive labor.

7.1.2 Universal Basic Services — The Foundation of Human Dignity

Nordic countries provide, free at point of use:

- healthcare

- education (including university)
- childcare
- eldercare
- unemployment benefits
- parental leave
- disability services
- housing assistance
- mental health support
- workforce retraining
- public transportation

In the AI era, when millions lose jobs to automation, this safety net becomes essential.

Nordic UBS ensures:

- survival is not tied to labor
- people can pursue education anytime
- workers can retrain without bankruptcy
- families can function without crushing costs
- innovation emerges from stability, not desperation

This is exactly what a post-labor society requires.

7.1.3 Strong Unions + Labor Protection — A Buffer Against Exploitation

Nordic unions:

- negotiate national wage agreements
- ensure fair working conditions
- coordinate with employers and government
- prevent corporate abuse
- maintain balanced economic power

Union membership can exceed 60–70% of workers.

In the AI era, where:

- capital becomes dominant
- labor bargaining power collapses
- job replacement accelerates
- workers lose leverage

unions become essential for managing the transition.

The Nordic model already has the structure for:

- negotiating automation timelines
- securing worker benefits
- shaping AI workplace policies
- integrating new technologies safely

This structure is missing in almost all other countries.

7.1.4 Trust + Low Inequality — The Secret Ingredient of Social Stability

Nordic societies have some of the lowest inequality on earth.

Low inequality produces:

- high social trust
- low crime
- low corruption
- high cooperation
- strong mental health
- civic pride
- faith in institutions
- willingness to pay taxes
- willingness to share resources

Trust is not decorative.
Trust is a foundation.

AI societies require massive redistribution of wealth.
Redistribution requires trust in the state.
Trust requires transparency and equality.

Nordic countries have this psychological foundation.
Most countries do not.

7.1.5 Transparency + Accountability — The Immune System of Democracy

Nordic countries score among the least corrupt nations in the world.

They enforce:

- transparency laws
- freedom of information
- strong investigative journalism
- citizen oversight
- independent anti-corruption bodies
- open public records
- strict limits on political donations

AI requires:
- complete algorithmic transparency
- public oversight
- accountability mechanisms

Because any government hiding its actions will misuse AI as a weapon of surveillance, censorship, or propaganda.

Transparency is non-negotiable.

Nordic institutions already embody this principle.

7.2 Why the Nordic Model Outperforms Both Capitalism and Authoritarianism

The 20th century framed global politics as:

Capitalism vs. Communism
USA vs. USSR
Markets vs. State

The 21st century reframes the debate:

Democratic Social Welfare vs. Authoritarian Capitalism
Nordic model vs. China model
Rights vs. Control
Transparency vs. Censorship
Dignity vs. Fear

The Nordic model is the only structure proven to produce:

- economic dynamism
- social equality

- political freedom
- long-term stability
- high innovation
- human well-being
- democratic legitimacy

These results are not random.
They arise from deep structural alignment with human nature.

Let us examine three reasons Nordic countries outperform all others.

7.2.1 Reason One: Safety Creates Freedom, Not Dependency

Critics say:

"Welfare makes people lazy."

Data says:

- Nordic workforce participation rates are among the highest in the world
- Productivity is strong
- Entrepreneurship is thriving
- Innovation indexes are world-leading

When survival is guaranteed, people dare to take risks.

When survival is fragile, people cling to stability.

Safety does not create dependency.
Safety creates freedom.

This is exactly what the AI future requires.

A society where:

- people explore
- people learn
- people innovate
- people pivot careers
- people invest in themselves
- people participate in democracy

Without fear of starvation.

7.2.2 Reason Two: Equality Maximizes Talent

In unequal societies:

- education quality varies
- opportunity depends on wealth
- children inherit disadvantage
- elites gatekeep access
- society wastes talent

The Nordic model invests heavily in:

- equal early education
- equal childcare
- equal public schools
- equal nutrition
- equal social conditions

The result:

maximum human potential unlocked.

A post-labor AI society will thrive only if:

- every citizen has equal access
- every mind is supported
- every opportunity is shared

Nordic countries already operate this way.

7.2.3 Reason Three: Transparent Institutions Reinforce Stability

Nordic countries trust institutions because institutions earn that trust.

This creates a stable cycle:
- Trust → cooperation
- Cooperation → stability
- Stability → innovation
- Innovation → prosperity

- Prosperity → equality
- Equality → more trust

Meanwhile, authoritarian systems create the opposite cycle:

- Fear → silence
- Silence → corruption
- Corruption → inequality
- Inequality → instability
- Instability → repression
- Repression → collapse

AI magnifies both cycles.

Only the Nordic cycle is sustainable.

7.3 Why the Nordic Model Is the Blueprint for the AI Era

The AI revolution does not simply modify society —
it *redefines* society.

AI forces humanity to confront questions:

- What happens when work disappears?
- How do we distribute wealth generated by machines?
- How do we maintain democracy when information becomes fluid?
- How do we ensure human dignity in a world of automation?
- How do we redesign the social contract?

Most countries are not prepared for these questions.
Their political systems, economic ideologies, and cultural norms are built on centuries-old assumptions:

- Work = survival
- Capital = power
- Markets = fairness
- Taxes = punishment
- Government = inefficiency
- Inequality = natural
- Labor unions = obstruction
- Social safety nets = laziness
- Public services = socialism

These assumptions collapse in the AI era.

Meanwhile, the Nordic model already embodies the values required for post-labor stability:

- redistribution
- public investment
- social trust
- rights-based dignity
- democratic accountability
- strong universal services
- transparent institutions
- low inequality
- high taxes to fund civilization

Let us examine why each of these features is essential for the future.

7.3.1 Redistribution Is Not Optional — It Is the Economic Engine of the AI Era

AI destroys:

- wage bargaining power
- middle-class security
- predictable careers
- employment-based identity
- labor's economic relevance

In this world:

wealth automatically concentrates

in the hands of those who own AI infrastructure.

Unless redistribution intervenes,
society collapses into neo-feudalism:

- AI billionaires as new lords
- the majority as surplus population
- social unrest, fragmentation, breakdown

Nordic countries already practice aggressive redistribution.
They tax:

- inheritance
- real estate speculation
- capital gains
- corporate profits
- high-income earners

and redistribute the proceeds into:

- education
- healthcare
- public housing
- childcare
- eldercare
- public transit
- unemployment systems
- social insurance

Redistribution is not a political preference.
It is the economic mechanism that prevents social collapse when machines replace workers.

Most countries have no such mechanism.
Nordic countries do.

7.3.2 Universal Services Are the Only Path to Post-Labor Stability

The AI era requires:

- free healthcare
- free education
- free lifelong learning
- free childcare
- free eldercare
- free mental healthcare
- affordable housing
- universal digital access
- public AI models
- basic income + social services

Nordic countries already have this infrastructure.
No other region on Earth is even close.

The U.S., for example:

- ties healthcare to employment
- charges university tuition that leads to massive debt
- underfunds public transit
- makes childcare unaffordable
- leaves workers exposed to layoffs
- denies many basic rights

This model collapses instantly in an AI world where jobs vanish overnight.

Nordic countries, by contrast, guarantee:

- you will not lose healthcare
- you will not lose education
- you will not lose shelter
- you will not lose dignity
- you will not lose access to society

even if you lose your job.

This is the future.

7.3.3 High Tax = High Civilization

The most important philosophical truth for the post-labor world:

Taxes are not a burden.

Taxes are the price of civilization.

Nordic countries treat taxes not as theft
but as *investment*:

- in trust
- in equality
- in public goods
- in social stability
- in human potential
- in innovation
- in long-term prosperity

The evidence is overwhelming:

Countries with high taxes:

- have more innovation
- have stronger economies
- have healthier populations
- have higher happiness
- have less crime
- have more stable democracies
- have more resilient societies
- weather crises better

Countries with low taxes:

- have fragile social safety nets
- have high inequality
- have polarized politics
- have weaker public institutions
- have lower social mobility
- experience more instability

The AI future intensifies this difference.

7.3.4 Low Inequality Is a Requirement for AI Stability

Inequality in the AI era is more dangerous than at any time in history.

Why?

Because inequality becomes permanent:

- capital compounds exponentially,
- AI multiplies capital returns,
- machines replace labor,
- wages stagnate or disappear,
- wealth concentrates into a tiny elite,
- social mobility collapses.

In the United States, inequality has become a national security threat.
In China, inequality threatens political legitimacy.
In developing countries, inequality causes brain drain and unrest.

Nordic countries maintain inequality at some of the lowest levels on Earth.
This is not accidental —
it is engineered through:

- high taxes
- strong unions
- universal benefits
- inheritance taxation
- housing policy
- labor protections
- transparent institutions

In the AI era, low inequality is not a moral ideal —
it is a survival requirement.

7.3.5 Trust Is the New Currency of Civilization

AI societies require trust because:

- algorithms shape our information
- governments will manage AI distribution
- citizens must accept redistribution
- institutions must oversee AI fairly
- political systems must remain stable

Most societies lack this trust due to:

- corruption
- inequality
- elite capture
- political polarization
- media manipulation
- propaganda
- historical trauma

The Nordic countries have the highest trust levels in the world.

People trust:

- the government
- the courts
- the healthcare system
- schools

- police
- unions
- media
- each other

This trust is not naive.
It is earned through:

- transparency
- accountability
- fairness
- open data
- anti-corruption norms
- shared prosperity

Trust is the psychological foundation of a post-labor society.

Without trust, redistribution collapses.
Without redistribution, AI civilization collapses.

7.3.6 Democracy + Welfare = The Best AI Governance System

Authoritarian systems collapse under AI pressure
(as explained in Chapters 5 and 6).

Hyper-capitalist systems collapse under inequality
(as explained in Chapters 3 and 4).

The Nordic model is the only system with:

- democratic legitimacy
- strong welfare state
- transparent governance
- open society
- economic dynamism
- cultural cohesion
- healthy public institutions

This combination is optimal for managing:

- AI benefits
- AI risks

- AI concentration
- AI oversight
- AI dividends
- AI-driven redistribution

Nordic countries already operate with a mindset that AI civilization requires:

- collective responsibility
- public oversight
- equal opportunity
- universal access
- moral leadership

The future will not be American capitalism.
The future will not be Chinese authoritarianism.

The future will be Nordic in structure, global in scale.

7.4 What the World Can Learn — Policy by Policy, System by System

The Nordic model is not culturally exclusive.
It is structurally replicable.

Any country can adopt its principles, adapted to local context.

Below are the most transferable lessons.

7.4.1 Lesson One: Health and Education Must Be Universal Rights

Nordic countries treat:

- healthcare
- education
- mental health
- childcare
- eldercare

as human rights.

Not as optional benefits.
Not as commodities.

Not as employer perks.

This aligns with the needs of the AI era:

If intelligence becomes free,

**then healthcare and education must also be free —
or inequality becomes catastrophic.**

Countries that do not adopt universal services
will face social collapse in the AI age.

7.4.2 Lesson Two: High Taxation Is Necessary to Maintain Freedom

Freedom without economic security is a myth.

Nordic citizens are free because their government guarantees:

- survival
- dignity
- stability

which allows:

- creativity
- risk-taking
- entrepreneurship

Countries that refuse to tax wealth heavily
will create:

- AI billionaires
- AI aristocracies
- extreme inequality
- social unrest
- political destabilization

High taxation is not a punishment.
It is engineering.

It builds the social infrastructure of freedom.

7.4.3 Lesson Three: Democracy Must Be Transparent and Accountable

Nordic democracies succeed because:

- corruption is low
- institutions are trusted
- citizens participate
- the press is independent
- law enforcement is professional
- courts are independent

AI demands even more transparency:

- open algorithmic audits
- ethical oversight boards
- citizen participation in AI policy
- public AI infrastructure

The future belongs to transparent democracies,
not opaque states.

7.4.4 Lesson Four: Work Culture Must Shift From Competition to Cooperation

Nordic workplaces are built on:

- cooperation
- equality
- team decision-making
- low hierarchy
- work-life balance
- flexible hours
- social responsibility

This culture aligns perfectly with AI, because:

- machines remove repetitive tasks
- creativity becomes the main value
- emotional intelligence becomes essential
- collaboration outperforms competition

Competitive individualism is outdated.
Cooperative innovation is the future.

Nordic culture is already there.

7.5 The Nordic Model vs. Authoritarian "Stability"

Authoritarian states often claim they provide stability, efficiency, and order, while democracies are slow, divided, and messy.

This argument collapses under close examination — especially in the AI era.

The Nordic model demonstrates that:

True stability comes from trust, equality, rights, and transparency —

not fear, surveillance, and coercion.

The contrast between these two models reveals why authoritarianism cannot survive the AI century, while the Nordic model can flourish.

7.5.1 Authoritarian "Stability" Is Actually Repression

Authoritarian regimes define stability as:

- absence of public protest
- absence of dissent
- absence of open criticism
- controlled media
- controlled information
- controlled elections
- controlled public institutions

But this is not stability.

This is fragile suppression, a frozen political ecosystem waiting to crack.

A society without protest is not peaceful.
It is voiceless.

A society without criticism is not unified.
It is fearful.

A society without elections is not stable.
It is stagnant.

Authoritarian stability is a facade maintained by:
- censorship
- propaganda
- political violence
- manufactured statistics
- fear of punishment

This model collapses under AI because:

- AI exposes lies,
- AI amplifies contradictions,
- AI reveals corruption,
- AI disrupts centralized control.

The Nordic model, by contrast, produces stability through:

- transparency
- shared prosperity
- democratic legitimacy
- strong institutions
- social trust
- low inequality

This is real stability —
resilient, adaptive, and sustainable.

7.5.2 Nordic Stability Is Built on Trust, Not Fear

Trust is the core of Nordic society.

People trust:

- government
- courts
- police
- media
- neighbors
- institutions

Trust arises because:

- transparency laws prevent secrecy
- public data is open
- corruption is punished
- inequality is low
- democracy is respected
- public services are universal
- elections are fair
- leaders are accountable

Contrast with authoritarian states, where:

- citizens distrust the government
- government distrusts citizens
- institutions distrust the public
- elites distrust one another
- society becomes paranoid
- information becomes weaponized

AI cannot operate in a distrust-based society.

Because AI requires:

- honest data
- open communication
- transparent feedback loops
- public oversight
- institutional integrity
- collaborative governance

Nordic trust makes AI adoption smooth and safe.
Authoritarian distrust makes AI adoption dangerous and corrupt.

7.5.3 Authoritarian Efficiency Is a Myth — It Is Actually Institutional Weakness

Authoritarian states claim they are efficient because:

- decisions are "fast"
- dissent is "removed"
- debate is "eliminated"
- orders are implemented immediately

But fast decisions do not mean good decisions.

In reality, authoritarian states suffer from:

- groupthink
- lack of feedback
- fear of reporting problems
- falsified data
- bureaucratic sycophancy
- corruption networks
- low creativity
- poor crisis management

Example:
During disasters, authoritarian systems fail because:

- lower-level officials hide the truth
- upper-level officials fear punishment
- no one takes responsibility
- real data never reaches leadership
- propaganda overrides logistics

The Nordic model, by contrast, thrives because:

- bad news can be reported
- criticism is expected
- mistakes are openly corrected
- institutions collaborate rather than compete
- transparency prevents systemic failure
- media exposes problems early
- accountability drives competence

This is the real meaning of efficiency in the 21st century.

AI systems magnify both strengths and weaknesses.

A transparent democracy improves faster with AI.
A closed authoritarian system collapses faster with AI.

7.5.4 Nordic Equality Leads to Long-Term Stability

Authoritarian regimes often tolerate — and even encourage — extreme inequality because:

- inequality creates dependency
- dependent citizens are easier to control
- elites benefit from inequality
- lack of social mobility prevents activism

But inequality is the deepest threat to AI civilizations.

Why?

Because AI replaces labor.

If wealth is not distributed, societies face:
- mass unemployment
- disappearance of middle class
- widespread poverty
- collapse of consumption
- political extremism
- violent instability

Nordic countries maintain low inequality through:

- progressive taxation
- universal services
- strong labor unions
- free education
- public housing options
- transparent institutions

This produces:

- social harmony
- predictable economic planning
- high mobility
- shared optimism
- stable democracies

AI thrives in equal societies.
AI destabilizes unequal societies.

This is why:

The future of AI governance looks Nordic, not authoritarian.

7.5.5 The Myth of Authoritarian Competence

Authoritarian propaganda often claims:

- "Our leaders are wise."
- "Our system is efficient."
- "Democracy is chaotic."
- "Western countries decline due to debate."

But competence cannot exist without:

- accountability
- transparency
- data integrity
- feedback loops
- free criticism

Authoritarian leaders surround themselves with:

- loyalists,
- sycophants,
- propagandists,
- corrupt administrators.

Their system cannot learn.
It cannot adapt.
It cannot correct itself.

AI will expose this incompetence:

- false statistics
- bad economic planning
- failed policies
- mismanaged crises
- unseen corruption

And once revealed, the regime loses legitimacy.

Nordic countries do not fear criticism —

they grow from it.

This is competence in the AI age.

7.6 Why the Nordic Structure Is the Closest Blueprint to the Utopia Humanity Society

The future civilization envisioned in this book — the Utopia Humanity Society — requires:

- heavy redistribution
- universal social services
- democratic transparency
- algorithmic oversight
- public ownership of intelligence
- AI dividends
- high progressive taxes
- human dignity guaranteed by institutions
- freedom not tied to labor
- deep equality as a foundation for innovation

These conditions already exist in Nordic societies, though not yet at AI-era levels.

Let's examine each requirement.

7.6.1 High Taxation and Redistribution as Civilizational Infrastructure

The Utopia Humanity Society requires:

- up to 80% taxation on extreme wealth
- redistribution of AI-generated wealth
- universal income
- universal services
- AI dividends

Nordic countries already embrace:

- high wealth taxes
- strong welfare state
- public investment

- robust social spending
- transparent redistribution

They are most compatible with the post-labor tax structure.

7.6.2 Universal Basic Services as a Foundation of Freedom

Nordic services include:

- healthcare
- education
- childcare
- eldercare
- transit
- disability support

and have nearly eliminated:

- medical bankruptcy
- unequal education opportunities
- severe poverty
- catastrophic life events

This aligns perfectly with AI society, where:

- careers shift rapidly
- job stability disappears
- retraining becomes constant
- survival must be guaranteed

The Utopia Humanity Society is impossible without strong public services.

Nordic countries already built them.

7.6.3 Transparency and Democratic Accountability

The Utopia Humanity Society requires:

- open-source public AI
- transparent governance
- algorithmic accountability
- civil rights protection

Nordic governments already:

- publish spending
- disclose records
- enforce anti-corruption
- protect press freedom
- operate with democratic legitimacy

This makes them ready to integrate Civic AI systems
that will manage:
- budgets
- policies
- welfare distribution
- public planning

in transparent and accountable ways.

Authoritarian systems cannot do this.

7.6.4 Low Inequality as the Psychological Foundation of Post-Labor Civilization

AI destroys labor markets and concentrates wealth.

Only societies with low inequality can:

- handle transition
- avoid social unrest
- maintain political stability
- preserve democratic legitimacy

Nordic societies already:

- minimize poverty
- maintain egalitarian norms
- reinforce solidarity
- invest in public goods

They have the social psychology needed to survive massive automation.

7.6.5 Human-Centered Culture: Cooperation Over Competition

The Utopia Humanity Society requires:

- empathy
- cooperation
- collective responsibility
- shared prosperity
- human dignity

Nordic culture already emphasizes:
- consensus
- inclusivity
- dialogue
- work-life balance
- emotional well-being
- community trust

This cultural foundation aligns naturally with post-labor philosophy.

The future cannot be built on aggressive competition.
It must be built on collaboration.

7.7 Closing: The Future Civilization Is Nordic at Its Core, Global in Its Expression

The world often looks to:

- Silicon Valley for innovation
- China for industrial scale
- Switzerland for precision
- Singapore for governance
- America for culture
- Japan for discipline

But for the long-term structure of human civilization
in the age of AI and automation,
the correct model is:

The Nordic System —
democratic, redistributive, transparent, rights-based, egalitarian, humane.

It is not culturally Scandinavian.
It is structurally universal.

Any nation can adopt:

- high tax + high trust
- universal services
- transparent institutions
- strong welfare
- democratic accountability
- low inequality
- strong labor protections
- public investment

Nordic countries are the prototype,
not the finished product.

The Utopia Humanity Society builds on their foundation:

- extending redistribution
- adding AI dividends
- adding universal basic income
- nationalizing AI infrastructure
- guaranteeing digital rights
- integrating Civic AI governance
- redesigning economic identity
- eliminating labor-based survival
- guaranteeing dignity for all

If capitalism was born in England,
and industrialization was perfected in Germany,
and digital technology was born in America,

the post-labor civilization will be born from the Nordic blueprint.

The future is:

- egalitarian
- redistributive
- democratic
- transparent
- human-centered
- cooperative

- sustainable
- AI-enabled
- post-capitalist
- post-authoritarian

The Nordic model is not the end.
It is the beginning.

It is the bridge between the world we inherited
and the world we must create.

CHAPTER 8: THE UTOPIA HUMANITY SOCIETY: CORE PRINCIPLES

A New Social Contract for the Age of AI, Abundance, and Human Dignity

The 20th century belonged to capitalism.
The 21st century will not.

Capitalism, as we inherited it, assumes:

- labor creates value,
- markets allocate resources,
- competition drives innovation,
- scarcity defines economics,
- growth requires inequality,
- low taxes increase prosperity,
- government intervention distorts efficiency.

All of these assumptions collapse in the age of artificial intelligence.

AI does not sleep.
AI does not demand wages.
AI does not strike.
AI does not require healthcare.
AI does not retire.
AI does not consume in the human sense.
AI produces value at near-zero marginal cost.

And most importantly:

AI does not distribute wealth.

Capitalism has no built-in mechanism to deal with:

- infinite productivity,
- zero labor cost,
- extreme concentration of capital,
- exponential wealth accumulation by a tiny elite
- massive unemployment,
- collapse of consumer demand,
- disappearance of the middle class.

Capitalism was designed for scarcity, not abundance.
For competition, not cooperation.
For human labor, not autonomous intelligence.

AI destroys the foundation of capitalism
not because capitalism is immoral,
but because capitalism is structurally incompatible
with laborless value creation.

The Utopia Humanity Society is the next step —
not utopian fantasy,
but the logical consequence of technological reality.

This chapter defines its core principles.

8.1 The First Principle: Dignity as a Birthright

Human dignity cannot depend on:

- employment,
- income,
- status,
- productivity,
- competition,
- obedience,
- corporate survival,
- market success.

These were the rules of the industrial age.
In the age of AI, they become obsolete — even cruel.

When machines can perform almost every economically valuable task,
tying dignity to labor becomes inhumane.

The Utopia Humanity Society begins with a radical but essential principle:

Every human being has inherent dignity

simply by being alive.

Dignity includes:

- healthcare
- education
- food
- housing
- safety
- social participation
- digital access
- mental health support
- community belonging

Dignity is not earned — it is guaranteed.

If AI can produce abundance,
then dignity must become universal.

8.2 The Second Principle: Freedom From Survival Anxiety

For 5,000 years, human societies operated under one brutal law:

Work or die.

Even modern capitalism never escaped this primal structure.

Lose your job → lose your healthcare.
Lose your job → lose your home.
Lose your job → lose your future.
Lose your job → lose your dignity.

AI exposes the madness of this model.

If machines do the work,
why must humans fight for survival?

The Utopia Humanity Society guarantees:

- a universal income floor,
- universal basic services,
- universal access to AI,
- universal access to public goods,
- protection against economic shocks,
- freedom to reinvent one's life without fear.

Freedom is not the ability to choose between brands.
Freedom is the ability to live without terror.

A society where basic needs are guaranteed
frees people to become:

- artists
- scientists
- entrepreneurs
- caregivers
- community builders
- thinkers
- inventors
- explorers
- creators

The purpose of life becomes self-actualization, not survival.

8.3 The Third Principle: Public Ownership of Intelligence

In the industrial era, the most important asset was capital — machines, factories, infrastructure.

In the AI era, the most important asset becomes intelligence.

If private corporations exclusively own:

- general AI models
- data pipelines
- automated production systems
- autonomous supply chains
- predictive analytics
- algorithmic governance tools

then society becomes dependent on:

- unaccountable platforms,
- wealth-concentrating algorithms,
- monopolistic power,
- corporate surveillance,
- private political influence.

This leads to AI feudalism —

a world where a handful of tech elites control wealth, information, and power.

To prevent this dystopia, the Utopia Humanity Society establishes:

Public ownership of foundational AI models,

while allowing private innovation on top.

This is similar to:

- public roads
- public libraries
- public education
- public electricity grids
- public water systems

Everyone can use them.
Everyone can build on top.
No one owns the foundation.

Public AI ensures:

- equal access
- equal opportunity
- transparent algorithms
- democratic oversight
- prevention of monopolies
- fair distribution of wealth

Without public AI, democracy dies.

8.4 The Fourth Principle: High Progressive Taxation as Civilizational Engineering

AI concentrates wealth at unprecedented levels.

Even under current capitalism,
we see the rise of:

- trillionaire candidates,
- billionaire dynasties,
- AI monopolies,

- extreme financialization,
- collapsing middle class.

In the AI era, this spirals out of control.

Without intervention:

- 0.1% will own nearly all productive assets
- AI-generated wealth goes to capital owners only
- unemployment rises
- consumption falls
- inequality explodes
- democracy collapses
- authoritarian populism rises
- social cohesion breaks
- economies stagnate
- political violence emerges

The Utopia Humanity Society prevents this outcome through:

Progressive taxation up to 80%

on extreme wealth and AI-driven profit concentration.

This is not punishment.
This is economic engineering.

High tax ensures:

- wealth recirculates
- public services remain funded
- universal income is sustainable
- AI dividends reach everyone
- inequality does not destabilize society
- political power is not captured by oligarchs
- long-term planning becomes possible

Nordic nations already prove this model works.

This is the tax architecture of the future.

8.5 The Fifth Principle: Universal Basic Services as the Foundation of Civilization

Universal Basic Services (UBS) include:

- healthcare
- education
- childcare
- eldercare
- public housing
- transit
- mental health
- disability support
- digital access
- public AI
- unemployment insurance
- workforce retraining

The Utopia Humanity Society adopts UBS as a civilizational right.

UBS creates:

- social stability
- equality of opportunity
- health security
- strong families
- higher innovation
- reduced inequality
- lower crime
- psychological well-being
- intergenerational mobility

Capitalism treats these as *costs*.
The Utopia Humanity Society treats them as the basic operating system of humanity.

When machines take over economic production,
human society must take responsibility for human flourishing.

8.6 The Sixth Principle: AI Dividends for Every Citizen

Every nation has:

- mineral wealth
- oil wealth
- land wealth
- water wealth
- intellectual property wealth
- sovereign wealth
- collective infrastructure

The 21st century adds a new category:

AI wealth —

value generated by machine intelligence using public data, public infrastructure, and public resources.

AI wealth belongs to the people.
Not corporations.
Not billionaires.
Not governments alone.

Every citizen becomes a shareholder of their nation's AI productivity.

AI dividends:

- fund basic income
- fund universal services
- fund public goods
- stabilize the economy
- reduce financial anxiety
- ensure dignity
- maintain democracy

When machines produce value,
humanity must share the profit.

This is how capitalism transitions into post-capitalism without collapse.

8.7 The Seventh Principle: Work Becomes Optional — Purpose Becomes Central

In the industrial world, work defined identity.

People asked:

"What do you do?"
"What is your job?"
"What career are you in?"

Work was a badge of worthiness.

AI destroys this identity structure.

The Utopia Humanity Society redefines the question:

Not "What is your job?"

but "What is your contribution to life?"

Work becomes:

- creative pursuit
- service
- invention
- exploration
- care
- craftsmanship
- expression
- innovation

Work loses its survival function
and becomes a self-actualizing function.

Humans evolve from economic units
to conscious beings with purpose.

This is the most profound transformation in human history.

8.8 The Eighth Principle: Transparency, Democracy, and Algorithmic Accountability

AI can strengthen or destroy democracy.

If AI remains in private hands,
it becomes a tool of manipulation and control.

If AI remains opaque,
it becomes a black box of unaccountable power.

The Utopia Humanity Society requires:

- open-source public AI
- algorithmic transparency
- privacy protection
- digital rights
- civic oversight
- participatory governance
- citizen assemblies
- transparent budgeting
- AI-assisted democratic decision-making

Democracy does not end with AI —
it evolves with AI.

AI becomes:

- a public servant
- not a master
- not a corporate tool
- not a state weapon

Democracy must modernize or die.
The UHS ensures it modernizes.

8.9 The Ninth Principle: Society as a Network of Care, Not a Marketplace of Survival

The industrial age taught us:

"Everyone for themselves."

"Competition makes us strong."
"Scarcity shapes virtue."
"Care is a private responsibility."

The Utopia Humanity Society reverses these assumptions.

A civilization built on abundance has different logic:

- care becomes a public value
- cooperation replaces competition
- empathy becomes necessary
- loneliness becomes a public concern
- mental health becomes civilizational infrastructure
- communities are rebuilt
- families receive support
- social bonds strengthen

Society becomes a network of care,
not a battlefield of individuals.

This is not softness —
it is advanced social engineering.

A connected society is a resilient society.

8.10 The Tenth Principle: Sustainability and Planetary Stewardship

AI accelerates the extraction of resources,
but it also enables:

- circular economies
- renewable infrastructures
- resource optimization
- regenerative agriculture
- precision environmental management

The Utopia Humanity Society integrates:

- carbon-neutral living
- zero-waste production
- sustainable architecture
- ecosystem restoration

- planetary-level monitoring

Humanity evolves from being:

- conquerors of nature

to

- custodians of nature.

This is the ecological dimension of dignity.

8.11 Why the Utopia Humanity Society Is NOT Communism,

NOT Socialism, and NOT Capitalism —
But a Fourth System Entirely

Whenever a new social system is proposed, people instinctively compare it to old categories:

- capitalism
- socialism
- communism
- social democracy
- anarchism

But the Utopia Humanity Society (UHS) does not fit any of them.
It is something historically unprecedented.

Communism failed because scarcity made equality impossible.

Capitalism is failing because AI makes labor irrelevant.

Socialism is incomplete because it relies on industrial structures.

Nordic social democracy is the transitional prototype — but not the final form.

UHS emerges from a technological reality the 20th century never imagined:

AI-driven abundance.

Once machines can produce goods and services at effectively zero marginal cost, entire categories of political ideology collapse.

This section explains why UHS is a new civilization model, not a recycled ideology.

8.11.1 Why UHS Is NOT Communism

Communism claims:

- abolition of private property,
- centralized planning,
- a vanguard party,
- class struggle,
- dictatorship of the proletariat,
- suppression of markets,
- one-party rule,
- forced collectivism.

The Utopia Humanity Society rejects all of this.

UHS does NOT:

- abolish private property
- abolish markets
- abolish entrepreneurship
- abolish democracy
- centralize planning
- rely on a ruling party
- suppress dissent
- use violence to maintain control

Communism failed because:

- it centralized power dangerously
- it eliminated incentives
- it created totalitarian systems
- it suppressed innovation
- it produced shortages
- it relied on propaganda and fear
- it consumed human freedom

UHS does the opposite.

The UHS is democratic, transparent, decentralized, and innovation-driven.

It keeps:

- private entrepreneurship
- private creativity
- open markets
- decentralized governance
- civic freedoms
- human-centered rights
- public accountability
- algorithmic transparency

UHS is not communism.
Communism suppresses human dignity.
UHS guarantees human dignity.

Communism destroys incentives.
UHS amplifies incentives through freedom from survival anxiety.

Communism centralizes authority.
UHS distributes authority across democratic and algorithmic systems.

Communism failed because it fought against human nature.
UHS succeeds because it works with human nature.

8.11.2 Why UHS Is NOT Capitalism

Capitalism assumes:

- private ownership of capital
- profit as the primary motive
- markets as resource allocators
- inequality as natural
- labor as the value creator
- competition as the mechanism of progress
- government as a minimal regulator

AI destroys every single one of these assumptions.

Capital is no longer scarce.
AI replicates itself and scales infinitely.

Labor is no longer the source of value.

AI generates value autonomously.

Markets fail under extreme inequality.
Consumer demand collapses when people have no income.

Competition becomes irrelevant.
The first AI to dominate a sector wins permanently.

Inequality becomes catastrophic.
A handful of people controlling AI could own the entire economy.

Wealth no longer flows to workers, only to asset owners.
This collapses consumption and destabilizes society.

Capitalism cannot survive when machines replace labor.
It becomes a self-destructive system:

- Productivity rises
- Wages fall
- Consumption collapses
- Profit shrinks
- Monopolies dominate
- Middle class disappears
- Democracy collapses

The UHS solves capitalism's contradictions through:

- AI dividends
- universal services
- public AI
- progressive taxation
- democratic oversight
- shared prosperity
- guaranteed dignity

Capitalism is about private gain.
UHS is about collective flourishing.

Capitalism is built on scarcity.
UHS is built on abundance.

Capitalism needs inequality to function.
UHS treats inequality as civilizational failure.

Capitalism treats human beings as economic inputs.
UHS treats human beings as ends in themselves.

8.11.3 Why UHS Is NOT Socialism

Socialism is broad, but generally involves:

- public ownership of major industries,
- expanded worker rights,
- strong labor unions,
- partial redistribution,
- regulated markets.

But socialism assumes an industrial economy, where:

- factories are labor-intensive
- productivity relies on workers
- unions negotiate wages
- public ownership improves bargaining power

However, in an AI-driven economy:

- factories need almost no workers
- productivity is machine-driven
- unions lose relevance
- ownership of industries does not guarantee fair distribution
- central planning breaks under data complexity

Socialism cannot handle:

- exponential AI-generated wealth
- zero marginal cost production
- AI monopolies
- post-labor identity
- data-driven societies

UHS goes far beyond socialist models:

UHS nationalizes only intelligence infrastructure,

not all industries.

Entrepreneurs still innovate.

Small businesses still thrive.
Creative ventures still flourish.
Markets still operate.
Competition still exists.

But the *foundation* — AI infrastructure — belongs to everyone.

UHS is not socialism.
It is a new structure built for a new technological era.

8.11.4 Why UHS Is the Fourth System — The Post-Labor Civilization

Humanity has gone through three economic stages:

1. Agrarian Civilization (5,000 BCE – 1800 CE)

- wealth = land
- power = landowners
- survival = farming
- inequality = extreme
- labor = physical

2. Industrial Civilization (1800–2000)

- wealth = capital + factories
- power = industrialists
- survival = wages
- inequality = class-based
- labor = mechanical / manufacturing

3. Information Capitalism (2000–2025)

- wealth = data + platforms
- power = tech monopolies
- survival = digital relevance
- inequality = global
- labor = cognitive

Now begins stage four:

4. Utopia Humanity Society (2025+)

The Post-Labor Civilization

Its characteristics:

- wealth = AI-generated value
- power = distributed through democratic AI
- survival = guaranteed through UBS + UBI
- inequality = minimized
- labor = optional
- dignity = universal
- purpose = self-determined
- governance = transparent + algorithmically assisted
- economy = zero-marginal-cost production
- markets = operate on top of public AI foundations

This is a civilizational shift as significant as:

- the invention of agriculture
- the industrial revolution
- the digital revolution

But deeper —
because it changes the meaning of human life.

The UHS is the first system in history
designed for a world where machines perform the majority of productive tasks.

It does not emerge from ideology.
It emerges from necessity.

The UHS is post-capitalist,
post-socialist,
post-authoritarian,
post-industrial,
post-scarcity.

It is not left or right.
It is not socialist or capitalist.
It is not conservative or progressive.

It is the first system built around abundance, not scarcity.

8.12 How AI Makes Utopia Practical (Not Idealistic)

People hear the word "utopia"
and think of fantasy, impractical dreams, idealism disconnected from reality.

But this is because, for thousands of years,
utopia was impossible.

Why?

Because:

- resources were scarce
- wealth had to be extracted from labor
- production required human effort
- inequality was structurally unavoidable
- economies required survival competition

Utopia was a dream that technology could not support.

AI changes this permanently.

8.12.1 AI Eliminates Scarcity in Key Sectors

AI-driven automation reduces the cost of:

- manufacturing
- transportation
- energy management
- logistics
- agriculture
- digital goods
- services
- knowledge work
- creative production
- administrative tasks

AI allows:

- factories to run autonomously
- supply chains to self-optimize
- design and R&D to accelerate

- medical diagnosis to scale globally
- education to become personalized
- transportation to become autonomous
- governance to run on transparent algorithms

When the cost of producing goods and services approaches zero, scarcity collapses — and with it, the foundation of old economic systems.

Utopia becomes engineering, not imagination.

8.12.2 AI Enables Redistribution Without Punishing Productivity

In capitalism, redistribution is seen as:

- harmful to growth
- disincentivizing work
- punishing innovation

This is because under capitalism:

- productivity = labor + capital
- removing capital or labor reduces output

In AI society:

- productivity = algorithms
- production cost = near zero
- scaling = infinite
- human labor = minimal

This means redistribution no longer harms growth.

You can tax:

- AI profits
- intellectual property
- data infrastructure
- capital gains
- platform monopolies

without shrinking productive capacity.

Redistribution becomes:

- efficient
- stable
- fair
- growth-neutral
- civilization-sustaining

This makes Utopia Humanity Society economically realistic.

8.12.3 AI Makes Universal Basic Services Affordable

Under capitalism, governments claim they "cannot afford":
- free healthcare
- free education
- public childcare
- affordable housing
- eldercare
- mental health services
- public transportation

But AI reduces the cost of all these services by:
- automating administration
- optimizing logistics
- accelerating discovery
- personalizing care
- reducing waste
- eliminating inefficiency

For example:

AI-assisted healthcare reduces:
- diagnosis costs
- administrative overhead
- error rates
- unnecessary testing
- patient wait times

AI-assisted education reduces:
- teacher workload
- curriculum cost

- tutoring inequality
- testing overhead

AI-assisted public planning reduces:

- corruption
- cost overruns
- project delays
- inefficiency

Utopia becomes practical when machines handle the cost structure.

8.12.4 AI Allows Humans to Redefine Purpose Beyond Survival

The real barrier to utopia has never been technology.
It has been psychology.

- fear
- scarcity
- competition
- insecurity
- survival pressure

AI frees humanity from these psychological chains.

When survival is guaranteed,
the human mind can evolve beyond:

- fear of failure
- tribal competition
- status anxiety
- insecurity
- economic desperation

Human purpose expands to:

- meaning
- creativity
- exploration
- contribution
- community
- spiritual development
- scientific advancement

- planetary stewardship

AI does not eliminate human purpose —
it liberates it.

8.12.5 AI Enables Transparent and Fair Governance

AI can:

- detect corruption
- flag fraud
- audit budgets
- identify bias
- evaluate policies
- optimize resource allocation

When combined with human oversight,
AI becomes a stabilizer of democracy.

It cannot replace democracy.
But it can strengthen it.

This makes UHS governance practical because:

- corruption becomes harder
- transparency becomes automatic
- inequality becomes visible
- justice becomes more consistent
- citizens become more empowered

AI brings clarity where politics once relied on manipulation.

CHAPTER 9: EXTREME PROGRESSIVE TAXATION (UP TO 80%)

AS CIVILIZATIONAL INFRASTRUCTURE

Why High Tax Is the Only Mechanism That Can Stabilize an AI Economy

For two hundred years, mainstream economics insisted:

- tax cuts = growth
- low taxes = innovation
- high taxes = punishment
- government redistribution = inefficiency

These ideas were shaped during:

- the industrial revolution,
- labor-based economies,
- scarcity-driven markets,
- capital-intensive production,
- slow technological progress.

They no longer apply.

AI shatters every assumption in the traditional tax philosophy.

In an economy where:

- machines replace labor,
- productivity detaches from wages,
- wealth concentrates into capital owners,
- AI scales infinitely,
- marginal production cost approaches zero,
- monopolies become natural outcomes,

taxation becomes the central engineering tool
for maintaining:

- democracy,
- stability,

- fairness,
- social cohesion,
- consumption,
- innovation,
- equality,
- human dignity.

This chapter explains why extreme progressive taxation — up to 80% for ultra-wealth and AI-generated profits — is not optional but structurally necessary for the survival of society.

9.1 Why Tax Philosophy Must Be Rewritten for the Age of AI

Traditional tax policy was designed for a world where:

- human labor produced value,
- markets allocated resources efficiently,
- competition drove innovation,
- companies needed workers,
- wages fueled demand.

In this world, governments argued:

- "Lower taxes attract investment."
- "Tax cuts stimulate hiring."
- "Reducing taxes boosts economic activity."

This logic collapses in the AI era.

AI does not respond to tax incentives.

AI does not need a tax break to work harder.
AI does not choose between countries.
AI does not relocate factories.
AI does not demand salaries.

AI simply operates.

When production is driven by algorithms,
the purpose of taxation transforms:

It is no longer about:

- funding government functions,
- redistributing income,
- providing public goods,
- stabilizing business cycles,

but about:

building the operating system of post-capitalist civilization.

9.2 Low Taxation Was Not a Prosperity Strategy — It Was Merely a Strategy for the Industrial Era

The world misunderstood why low taxes helped economic growth in the 20th century.

Here is the real reason:

Low taxes increased capital accumulation at a time when capital investment created jobs.

Factories needed workers.
More capital → more jobs.
More jobs → more consumption.
More consumption → more growth.
More growth → more tax revenue.

It was a simple, mechanical loop.

But the loop breaks with AI.

Today:

- increased capital investment does NOT translate into jobs

- increased automation reduces hiring
- increased productivity does NOT increase wages
- consumption shrinks because labor income shrinks
- inequality explodes
- political instability rises

Low taxes accelerate the collapse of demand.

Low taxes starve governments of revenue needed to stabilize society.

Low taxes supercharge monopolies.

Low taxes accelerate wealth concentration.

Low taxes weaken democracy.

The idea that low taxes drive prosperity is not only outdated —
it becomes dangerous in the AI era.

9.3 Why Extreme Progressive Taxation Stabilizes an AI Economy

Extreme progressive taxation (e.g., 60%–80% on ultra-wealth, capital gains, AI profit concentration) serves several civilizational functions.

Function 1: Preventing AI-driven hyper-monopolies

AI naturally leads to winner-take-all dynamics:
- The best model → controls the sector
- The best dataset → dominates the economy
- The best infrastructure → owns the future

Without heavy taxation:
- one AI company could dominate the entire global economy
- a handful of trillionaires could own all productive capacity
- democracy would collapse under oligarchic control

Extreme taxation prevents:
- runaway capital concentration,
- financial aristocracy,
- corporate feudalism.

It forces wealth to recirculate.

Function 2: Funding Universal Basic Services (UBS)

Healthcare
Education
Childcare
Eldercare
Housing
Transportation
Digital access
AI access
Mental health care
Environmental protections

All require stable revenue streams.

AI-driven economies produce enormous profits
but concentrated in a tiny elite.

High progressive taxation ensures:
- UBS becomes sustainable
- every citizen receives services independent of employment
- social stability is maintained
- long-term planning is possible

UBS is not welfare.
UBS is civilization infrastructure.

Function 3: Funding Universal Basic Income (UBI)

When AI replaces labor:

- wage income collapses
- consumer demand falls
- economic cycles become unstable

UBI replaces wage income as the foundation of consumption.

Extreme progressive taxation creates:

- a steady revenue base
- a predictable national dividend
- a universal right to dignity

UBI is what maintains:

- market demand
- social harmony
- economic participation
- political stability

in a labor-minimized economy.

Function 4: Funding AI Dividends

AI uses:

- public data
- public research
- public infrastructure
- public resources
- public legal and educational systems

to generate value.

Therefore, AI profits must return to the people.

High taxation ensures:

- national AI dividends
- every citizen shares in the value
- corporations cannot extract wealth without limits

This is how AI becomes a public good.

Function 5: Preventing a Neo-Feudal Society

Without extreme taxation, the AI economy becomes:

- lord → AI owner
- serf → society
- castle → data centers
- land → digital infrastructure

This is neo-feudalism.

It is the natural outcome of:

- AI monopolies
- platform dominance
- intellectual property concentration
- weak public institutions
- low taxation
- deregulation
- private control of intelligence

High taxation is what prevents:

- hereditary AI dynasties
- multi-century wealth concentration
- political classes insulated by capital
- corporate takeover of democracy

Extreme tax is not punishment.
It is anti-feudal engineering.

Function 6: Preventing Collapse of Democracy

Democracy fails when:

- inequality rises
- the middle class disappears
- elite capture grows
- political polarization increases
- corporate power becomes unchecked

High taxation:

- restores the middle class
- funds public goods
- stabilizes society
- protects democracy
- limits oligarchy
- keeps power distributed

Democracy is not sustained by voting alone.
Democracy is sustained by economic equality.

9.4 Why 80% Taxation Is Rational — Not Radical

People react emotionally to high tax rates, but emotionally is not intellectually.

Consider this truth:

In the AI era, 80% taxation on extreme wealth still leaves the ultra-wealthy richer than any humans in history.

If someone earns:

- $10 billion → they keep $2 billion
- $1 billion → they keep $200 million
- $100 million → they keep $20 million
- $10 million → they keep $2 million

And for ordinary income earners:

- low and middle taxes stay low
- only extreme wealth is taxed heavily
- consumption power increases
- cost of living decreases through UBS
- entire society rises together

High taxation does not punish entrepreneurs —
it prevents oligarchs from replacing governments.

9.5 Why "Tax Cuts" Are Old School and Harmful in an AI Economy

Tax cuts were designed for:

- labor-based productivity
- industrial growth cycles
- pre-automation markets

But in the AI era, tax cuts:

- do not create jobs
- do not stimulate demand
- do not encourage innovation
- do not attract meaningful investment
- do not increase competitiveness
- do not improve equality
- do not stabilize economies

Tax cuts pull oxygen out of the public system.

Tax cuts weaken governments at the exact moment they need strength.

Tax cuts amplify inequality.

Tax cuts split society into elite vs. everyone else.

Tax cuts create unstable politics.

Tax cuts destroy public infrastructure.

Tax cuts belong to a dead era.

9.6 The Formula for Civilizational Stability

Let's define the structure mathematically.

Old Equation (Industrial Capitalism):

Growth = Capital Investment + Labor Productivity
New Equation (AI Civilization):

Stability = Redistribution + Universal Services + Public AI + Democratic Oversight

This is the heart of the UHS.

Extreme progressive taxation is the fuel for the entire system.

Without it, the machine stops.

9.7 Why the Nordic Model Proves Extreme Taxation Works

Nordic countries already tax:

- high incomes
- capital gains
- wealth
- inheritance
- corporate profits

at some of the highest rates globally.

The results:

- highest trust

- lowest inequality
- highest innovation per capita
- healthiest populations
- strongest democracies
- happiest citizens
- most stable economies

The Nordic model is the prototype,
but the UHS version of taxation goes further:

- taxing AI monopolies
- taxing automation profits
- taxing intellectual property
- taxing data wealth
- taxing algorithmic value extraction

This is the next layer of progressive taxation.

9.8 The Moral Foundation of UHS Taxation

Extreme taxation is not simply economic necessity.
It is a moral responsibility.

If AI can produce infinite wealth,

**then allowing a tiny elite to own that wealth
is a violation of human dignity.**

Wealth must circulate.
Prosperity must be shared.
AI must serve humanity, not the elite.
Technology must uplift everyone, not enslave.

High taxation is the mechanism
through which civilization honors:

- dignity
- fairness

- human potential
- community
- democracy
- justice

This is not redistribution for charity.
This is redistribution for civilizational survival.

9.9 The Tax Architecture of the Utopia Humanity Society

(Exact Models, Rates, and Mechanisms)

The Utopia Humanity Society is a complete re-engineering of how a civilization funds itself.
This requires a new tax architecture — not incremental reforms, but a structural redesign of:

- what is taxed,
- how it is taxed,
- why it is taxed,
- and how the revenue flows back into society.

This section outlines the precise tax design that stabilizes a post-labor, AI-driven society.

9.9.1 The Guiding Philosophy of UHS Taxation

The tax design rests on five principles:

1. Tax what machines produce, not what humans earn.

Human labor becomes less central.
Human dignity becomes more important.
Taxation must move from income → capital → automation → AI profits.

2. Tax extreme wealth, not ordinary life.

The middle class should be taxed lightly.
Extreme wealth is taxed heavily because extreme wealth becomes extreme power.

3. Tax monopolies more than competition.

AI tends toward monopoly.
Monopolies distort democracy.
Thus, monopolistic profits are taxed aggressively.

4. Tax negative externalities (pollution, extraction), not essential goods.

Preserve the environment.
Support sustainable consumption.

5. Direct tax revenue into universal services + AI dividends.

Revenue is not hoarded by the government — it flows back to:

- UBI
- UBS
- AI dividends
- public AI systems
- environmental restoration
- long-term infrastructure

This creates a closed-loop, self-reinforcing civilization model.

9.9.2 The UHS Tax Framework Overview

The UHS employs five major tax pillars:

Pillar 1: Extreme Progressive Income Taxation (50%–80% on ultra-high income)

This includes:

- salaries over $5 million
- bonuses over $2 million
- stock-based compensation
- financial-sector short-term gains
- excessive executive compensation

Tax brackets:

- 0% for the poor
- 10–25% for working and middle class
- 35% for upper-middle earnings
- 50% for high earners
- 65% for top 0.1%
- 80% for top 0.01%

This reverses the last 40 years of wealth concentration.

Pillar 2: AI Automation Tax (30%–60% of machine-generated value)

This is the most important new tax.

When companies replace labor with AI,
the value produced by machines must be taxed.

This includes:

- automated factories
- AI production pipelines
- AI customer service
- AI programming assistants
- AI logistics management
- robotic warehouses
- autonomous transportation

- algorithmic financial trading
- AI content creation
- AI administrative workflows

Mechanism:

- Calculate revenue generated from automated systems
- Deduct operational cost of running AI
- Tax the remaining automated productivity at 30–60%

This recycles wealth back into society.

Without this tax, automation benefits only the owners of machines.

Pillar 3: AI Monopoly Windfall Tax (60%–90%)

AI creates extreme winners:

- the best model wins everything
- the best data wins everything
- the most compute wins everything

This leads to:

- trillion-dollar companies
- global monopolies
- unaccountable corporate power
- political capture
- economic instability

The UHS introduces:

AI Monopoly Tax: 60%–90% on profits derived from monopoly position.

Criteria:

- market share over 60%
- algorithmic dominance

- control of essential infrastructure
- exclusive access to unique data

This ensures no single company becomes more powerful than the state.

Pillar 4: Wealth Tax (2–5% annually on net wealth above $50 million)

Wealth amplifies itself autonomously.

Even without work, wealth:

- earns interest
- increases in asset value
- multiplies through investment
- compounds exponentially

Meanwhile, those without capital fall behind permanently.

Thus, the UHS employs:

- 2% annual tax on wealth above $50 million
- 3% annual tax above $100 million
- 5% annual tax above $1 billion

This slows runaway accumulation and funds basic services.

Pillar 5: Data Dividend Tax (5–15% of corporate profits derived from public data)

Corporations profit immensely from:

- user data
- national datasets
- public health information
- satellite data
- internet behavior
- government-funded research

- academic scientific output

Public data is a public asset.

Mechanism:

- Companies pay 5–15% of profits derived from public datasets
- Funds are redistributed as national AI dividends

This ensures citizens benefit directly from their data.

9.9.3 Special AI-Era Taxes the UHS Introduces

The following taxes exist nowhere in the world yet,
but they become essential in the AI era.

A. Algorithmic Value Extraction Tax (AVET)

Whenever algorithms extract value from:

- user behavior
- consumer attention
- predictive analytics
- content optimization

an AVET tax applies.

Rate: 5–20% depending on extraction intensity.

Purpose:

- Prevent predatory algorithms
- Fund mental health and digital education
- Reduce manipulation and disinformation
- Support public-interest AI models

B. Digital Asset Accumulation Tax

For individuals or corporations holding massive digital assets:

- domain monopolies
- platform user bases
- exclusive data rights
- compute infrastructure

Rate: 1–3% annually on the value of these digital assets.

Purpose:
Prevent dominance of digital infrastructure by a tiny elite.

C. Sovereign Compute Tax

AI models require massive compute:

- GPUs
- TPUs
- ASICs
- data centers
- energy-intense processing

The UHS introduces a modest compute tax of:

- 0.5–2% of the capital cost of compute
- earmarked for public AI infrastructure

This prevents exclusive access to compute by corporations.

D. Autonomous Supply Chain Tax

Automation in logistics erases millions of jobs.

Taxing:

- autonomous trucks

- robotic warehouses
- AI logistics management systems
- automated ports

Rate: 20–40% of the wage-equivalent value replaced.

This tax funds UBI + retraining.

9.9.4 Redirecting Tax Revenue Into Civilizational Systems

All revenue flows into:

A. Universal Basic Services (UBS)

- healthcare
- education
- childcare
- eldercare
- mental health
- public housing
- transit
- digital access
- public AI

B. Universal Basic Income (UBI)

A guaranteed monthly payment to every citizen.

C. National AI Dividend

A payment tied specifically to the profitability of national AI systems.

D. Public AI Infrastructure

- national models
- transparent algorithms
- citizen-accessible AI tools

E. Environmental Regeneration

- carbon capture
- reforestation
- ocean cleanup
- renewable energy

F. Civic Strengthening

- media independence
- algorithmic oversight boards
- anti-corruption agencies
- public oversight platforms

This is how taxation transforms into civilizational architecture.

9.9.5 Why UHS Taxation Creates More Innovation, Not Less

This is the surprising truth:

High taxes increase innovation.

Why?

1. High taxes fund education and research.
Nordic countries have:

- world-leading education
- world-leading innovation per capita
- massive public investment in research

2. High taxes reduce survival anxiety.
People dare to:

- start companies
- take risks
- innovate
- fail safely
- invent new models

3. High taxes prevent monopolies.
Monopolies kill innovation.
Distributed wealth spreads experimentation.

4. High taxes fund universal basic income.
UBI increases:

- creativity
- entrepreneurship
- artistic exploration
- early-stage experimentation

Creativity thrives under security, not desperation.

9.9.6 Why UHS Taxation Makes the Middle Class Stronger

Under capitalism, taxes often weaken the middle class.
Under UHS, taxes strengthen it.

Here's why:

- middle-class taxes are low
- living expenses drop dramatically
- UBS eliminates major financial burdens
- UBI supplements income
- AI dividends boost purchasing power
- inequality decreases
- access to services increases

Middle-class life becomes:

- more stable
- less stressful
- more prosperous
- less precarious

Taxation, funded by wealth and AI, becomes a middle-class engine.

9.9.7 Practical Example: A Day in the Life Under UHS Taxation

Imagine a single mother living in a UHS country.

Her costs:

- Healthcare = free
- Childcare = free
- Schooling = free
- Transit = free
- Mental health services = free
- Housing support = available
- AI education tools = free
- UBI = monthly guaranteed
- AI dividends = annual payments

Her taxes?
- 15–20% of her income.

Meanwhile, a billionaire pays:

- 80% on extreme income
- 5% annual wealth tax
- 60% AI monopoly tax
- algorithmic extraction taxes
- automation taxes

The system becomes:

- fair
- stable
- dignified
- future-proof

This is civilization re-engineered.

9.9.8 Why This System Prevents Revolutions, Collapse, and Authoritarianism

History shows:

When inequality becomes extreme, societies collapse.

People revolt.
Populists rise.
Democracy disintegrates.
Authoritarianism takes over.

Extreme progressive taxation prevents:

- oligarchic takeover
- political destabilization
- fascism
- corruption
- elite capture
- civil unrest

It ensures:

- shared prosperity
- dignified living
- stable democracy
- long-term peace

Taxation becomes the immune system of civilization.

9.10 Global Case Study:

Why High-Tax Countries Outperform Low-Tax Countries (Economically, Socially, Politically, and in the AI Era)

For decades, politicians, economists, and business elites repeated a simple slogan:

"Low taxes create prosperity. High taxes destroy growth."

This was never true — but the illusion survived because:

- the U.S. had unique geographic advantages
- Europe rebuilt from Marshall Plan investments
- globalization allowed exploitation of cheap labor
- fossil fuel expansion created artificial wealth
- weak regulation enabled financial speculation

The myth collapses instantly once we compare:

High-Tax Countries vs. Low-Tax Countries

across:

- innovation
- entrepreneurship
- happiness
- productivity
- inequality
- public health
- political stability
- education
- AI readiness

The data points overwhelmingly in one direction:

High-tax societies outperform low-tax societies on every metric that matters for the AI century.

This section presents the evidence.

9.10.1 High-Tax Nordic Countries vs. Low-Tax Anglo-American Model

Let's compare:

High-tax Nordic countries

(Sweden, Denmark, Norway, Finland, Iceland)

versus

Low-tax nations

(USA, UK, Singapore, Hong Kong)

Using 12 critical indicators for the AI future.

Indicator 1 — Innovation

Nordic countries (with 50–60% tax rates) rank consistently top 10 globally in innovation per capita.

USA and UK rank high, but in innovation per capita, the Nordics outperform.

Why?

- their populations are highly educated
- healthcare is universal (people can innovate without fear)
- failure is not punished with bankruptcy
- governments fund R&D aggressively
- strong social safety nets allow risk-taking

Conclusion:

High taxes = more innovation, not less.

Indicator 2 — Entrepreneurship

Counterintuitive but true:

Nordic countries have *more entrepreneurs per capita* than the U.S.

Why?

Because in the Nordics:

- losing your job is not catastrophic
- healthcare does not disappear
- bankruptcy is not life-destroying
- childcare is affordable
- education is free
- failure is survivable

Entrepreneurship thrives where stability exists.

Conclusion:

Economic security creates entrepreneurial bravery.

Indicator 3 — Economic Productivity

Nordic productivity is among the highest in the world — often exceeding the U.S.

Because:
- healthy workers are more productive
- educated workers are more skilled
- society wastes less talent
- unions coordinate efficient wage structures
- public services reduce stress and absenteeism

Conclusion:

High taxes fuel high productivity.

Indicator 4 — Inequality

Nordic countries have some of the lowest inequality on Earth.

The U.S., UK, and low-tax countries have the highest.

Inequality is a disaster for the AI era because:
- consumer demand collapses
- social unrest increases
- democracy destabilizes
- elites capture political power
- public trust erodes

Conclusion:

High taxes protect democracy. Low taxes destroy it.

Indicator 5 — Happiness and Life Satisfaction

Every global ranking shows:

The top 10 happiest countries in the world are almost always high-tax Nordic nations.

People are happier because:
- their needs are guaranteed
- stress is lower
- public systems function
- work-life balance is healthier
- communities are stronger

Conclusion:

Taxation buys happiness by eliminating unnecessary suffering.

Indicator 6 — Crime and Social Stability

Countries with:
- universal services
- low inequality

- strong welfare
- strong unions
- public trust

have far less crime.

Nordic countries have some of the lowest crime rates on Earth.

Meanwhile, low-tax societies struggle with:
- mass incarceration
- violent crime
- drug epidemics
- homelessness
- social fragmentation

Conclusion:

High taxes create stability. Low taxes create chaos.

Indicator 7 — Education Quality

Nordic countries provide:
- free education
- highly paid teachers
- equitable school funding
- universal early childhood education

Their students consistently outperform global averages.

Low-tax countries like the U.S. have:
- massive student debt
- unequal schools
- unstable funding
- low teacher wages

Conclusion:

High taxes produce smarter societies.

Indicator 8 — Healthcare Outcomes

Nordic healthcare systems outperform the U.S. on:
- life expectancy
- infant mortality
- preventable deaths
- mental health
- cost efficiency

And they spend half as much per capita.

Why?

Because high-tax societies fund prevention, not profit.

Conclusion:

High taxes create healthier populations at lower cost.

Indicator 9 — Gender Equality

Nordic countries rank highest globally in:
- women's workforce participation
- workplace equality
- political representation
- parental leave benefits
- childcare affordability

Low-tax countries rank significantly lower.

Why does this matter for AI society?

Because gender equality:
- increases economic productivity

- stabilizes families
- expands workforce creativity
- improves social cohesion
- enhances democracy

Conclusion:

Gender equality thrives under high taxation and universal services.

Indicator 10 — Political Stability

Nordic countries consistently rank among the most:
- stable
- peaceful
- democratic
- corruption-free
- trusted

Low-tax societies experience:
- political polarization
- elite capture
- corruption
- populist extremism
- institutional decline

Conclusion:

High tax is political immunity. Low tax is democratic decay.

Indicator 11 — Public Trust

Trust is the most valuable currency in an AI society.

The Nordic world is high-trust because:
- institutions function
- people feel protected

- inequality is low
- transparency is enforced
- corruption is minimal

Low-tax societies are low-trust because:
- public services fail
- corruption is rampant
- inequality is high
- government is seen as incompetent
- institutions are weak

Conclusion:

High taxes build trust → trust stabilizes AI governance.

Indicator 12 — AI Readiness

Nordic countries are uniquely prepared for the AI era:
- strong welfare states stabilize displaced workers
- high education levels accelerate AI adoption
- universal digital access ensures equality
- public trust smooths transitions
- low inequality prevents social breakdown
- high taxes fund retraining + AI infrastructure

Meanwhile, low-tax societies face:
- mass job displacement
- institutional fragility
- corporate capture of AI
- lack of safety nets
- social unrest
- political chaos

Conclusion:

The AI era belongs to high-tax, high-trust societies.

9.10.2 Why High-Tax Economies Grow Faster Than Low-Tax Economies (Long-Term)

Contrary to neoliberal ideology, high-tax economies outperform low-tax ones in sustainable *long-term* growth.

Why?

1. High taxes fund education → educated societies grow faster.

2. High taxes fund healthcare → healthy workers are more productive.

3. High taxes fund public infrastructure → economies become more efficient.

4. High taxes reduce inequality → consumer demand increases.

5. High taxes stabilize society → businesses thrive in predictability.

6. High taxes fund research → innovations multiply.

7. High taxes reduce crime → communities flourish.

8. High taxes increase trust → economic friction decreases.

Meanwhile, low-tax economies suffer from:
- weak public services
- high inequality
- unstable politics
- poor education
- vulnerable healthcare systems
- social conflict
- financial crises

Short-term "growth" from low taxes is an illusion.
Long-term results are disastrous.

9.10.3 Why High Taxation Is the Only Sustainable Response to AI

AI creates:
- extreme productivity
- extreme concentration
- extreme inequality
- extreme disruption

Only high taxation can:
- redistribute wealth
- stabilize society
- fund universal services
- finance UBI
- regulate AI
- prevent monopolies
- preserve democracy

The alternative is:
- AI feudalism
- oligarch capture
- collapse of the middle class
- social unrest
- authoritarian takeover

High taxation is not ideology.
High taxation is structural engineering for a dignified future.

9.10.4 Why Corporations Actually Prefer High-Tax Societies (Secret Truth)

Executives don't admit this publicly, but research shows large corporations prefer:
- stable societies
- educated workers
- strong infrastructure
- predictable political climates
- healthy consumers

- low crime
- good public healthcare
- high levels of trust

These conditions exist in high-tax societies, not low-tax ones.

Low-tax societies:
- break down
- polarize
- become unstable
- create violent cycles
- lose talent
- lose global competitiveness

Corporations quietly know:

They thrive best when society thrives.

9.10.5 Why High Taxation Reduces Corruption

In low-tax societies:
- public institutions are weak
- politicians rely on private donors
- corporations buy influence
- regulation is captured
- enforcement is underfunded

In high-tax societies:
- governments are strong
- regulation is effective
- oversight is funded
- corruption is punished
- transparency is enforced

This is essential for AI governance.
AI requires:

- transparent oversight
- ethical auditing
- secure public infrastructure
- responsible deployment

Low-tax societies cannot manage AI safely.

9.10.6 Conclusion:

High Taxation Is the Only Model That Survives the AI Century

The choice is simple:

**High tax + universal dignity + strong public institutions
Or Low tax + collapse of democracy + AI feudalism.**

Every global trend confirms this:
- inequality is rising
- labor is disappearing
- monopolies are consolidating
- traditional economics is breaking
- political instability is spreading
- AI accelerates all of it

But high-tax societies:
- remain stable
- remain prosperous
- remain democratic
- remain innovative
- remain humane

The 21st century belongs to:
- the high-tax world
- the Nordic model
- the Utopia Humanity Society

Low-tax systems are relics of the industrial past.

They cannot survive the AI future.

9.11 Addressing Every Objection to High Taxation

(Growth, Innovation, Incentives, Freedom, Competitiveness)

Any time high taxation is proposed, five objections arise:
1. "High taxes kill growth."
2. "High taxes kill innovation."
3. "High taxes make people lazy."
4. "High taxes reduce freedom."
5. "High taxes push the wealthy to leave."

These arguments come from:
- 20th-century economics
- neoliberal ideology
- corporate propaganda
- outdated assumptions
- intentional misinformation

In the AI-driven 21st century, each of these objections becomes factually wrong and structurally obsolete.

This section dismantles each objection, one by one, with evidence, logic, and global comparisons.

OBJECTION 1

"High taxes kill economic growth."

This is the most common argument —
and the most easily disproven.

Fact:

The highest-taxed countries in the world (Nordic countries) consistently outperform low-tax countries in:

- productivity
- innovation
- human development
- social stability
- education
- health outcomes
- workforce participation
- per capita GDP growth

Meanwhile, low-tax societies like:

- the U.S.
- U.K.
- Singapore (for elites)
- Hong Kong

struggle with:

- inequality
- underfunded public services
- institutional instability
- social fragmentation
- mass homelessness
- declining life expectancy
- declining education performance

Taxation is not the enemy of growth.
Inequality is the enemy of growth.

High taxes → strong public systems → strong economy.
Low taxes → weak public systems → unstable economy.

AI Era Conclusion:

Economic growth depends on social stability and human dignity — both funded by high taxes.

OBJECTION 2

"High taxes kill innovation."

The evidence shows the opposite.

Innovation thrives in high-tax societies.

Why?

1. High taxes fund world-class education.

Innovation requires talent.
Talent requires education.
Education requires public investment.

2. High taxes fund research and development.

The internet, GPS, mRNA vaccines, AI algorithms —
all were funded by government spending, not private capital.

3. High taxes reduce personal risk.

When healthcare, childcare, and education are guaranteed:

- people start companies more easily
- failure is survivable
- creativity expands
- more people become entrepreneurs

The highest entrepreneurship-per-capita rates are in...
Nordic countries — not low-tax countries.

4. High taxes prevent monopolies that kill innovation.

Innovation dies when:

- one company dominates
- platforms lock out competition

215

- startups cannot enter the market

High taxes break monopolistic power.

5. AI-driven economies require state-led coordination.

Without high public investment:

- AI infrastructure becomes private
- innovation becomes captured by corporations
- public progress stagnates

AI Era Conclusion:

Innovation requires strong public foundations, not tax cuts for the wealthy.

OBJECTION 3

"High taxes make people lazy."

This argument assumes:

- people only work for survival
- people are naturally unproductive
- humans would do nothing if not forced
- the threat of poverty is necessary

These assumptions are psychologically false and ethically primitive.

Nordic countries — with high taxes and strong welfare —
have some of the highest workforce participation rates in the world.

Why?

1. People work more when they are healthy.

Healthcare increases productivity.

2. People work more when childcare is provided.

Parents can remain in the workforce.

3. People work more when education is free.

Skills are updated continuously.

4. People work more when mental health is supported.

Depression, anxiety, and burnout reduce economic participation.

5. People work more when jobs offer dignity.

Work becomes meaningful, not survival-driven.

6. People work differently in post-labor societies.

Work becomes:

- creative
- purposeful
- participatory
- flexible
- community-driven
- innovation-focused

People do not become lazy.
People become free.

AI Era Conclusion:

Humans seek meaning naturally — work becomes better when survival is not at stake.

OBJECTION 4

"High taxes reduce individual freedom."

This framing is a trick.

Low-tax countries say:

- "We give you freedom from taxes."

But what does that "freedom" cost?

In the U.S., low taxes lead to:

- $300,000 average lifetime healthcare cost
- $100,000+ student debt
- $15,000–$25,000 childcare costs per year
- unaffordable rent
- bankruptcy risk
- medical debt
- unstable employment
- fear-based living

This is not freedom.
This is *economic imprisonment.*

Real freedom is the freedom from fear.

High-tax societies provide:

- free healthcare
- free education
- free childcare
- affordable housing
- dignified eldercare
- mental health support
- universal digital access
- strong public transit
- stable income

- social trust

This is freedom you can *feel*.

High taxes create freedom. Low taxes create insecurity.

In the UHS, freedom becomes:
- freedom from poverty
- freedom from bankruptcy
- freedom from medical fear
- freedom from unemployment anxiety
- freedom to learn
- freedom to create
- freedom to build the life you want

AI Era Conclusion:

Freedom is not low tax. Freedom is guaranteed dignity.

OBJECTION 5

"High taxes push the wealthy to leave."

Another myth.

Data shows:
- wealthy people rarely leave high-tax countries
- moving is emotionally and operationally difficult
- their businesses, networks, and culture keep them anchored
- lifestyle quality matters more than marginal tax rates
- high-tax countries have better public goods
- wealthy individuals benefit from societal stability

Even when some wealthy individuals relocate:
- the gains from redistribution far exceed the losses from departure

- the social benefits outweigh individual exits
- high-tax countries remain stable and prosperous

Nordic Example:

Despite high taxes:

- billionaires stay
- millionaires stay
- entrepreneurs stay
- corporations stay

Why?

Because:

- society is stable
- corruption is low
- institutions are strong
- public services are excellent
- citizens are well-educated
- workforce is highly capable
- infrastructure is world-class

Wealthy people prefer predictable, safe, functional societies.

Those are created by high taxes.

Even if some ultra-rich individuals leave,
the system remains vastly more stable.

AI Era Conclusion:

A functioning society is more important than keeping every billionaire happy.

OBJECTION 6

"High taxes make countries uncompetitive."

This is only true for:

- financial speculation
- tax evasion industries
- corporate rent-seeking
- resource extraction barons

But for real competitiveness — innovation, education, stability — high-tax societies outperform.

Consider the global competitiveness index:

- Norway
- Denmark
- Sweden
- Finland
- Netherlands
- Germany

All high-tax, high-regulation countries.

Why competitive?

Because:

- talent is abundant
- education is world-class
- inequality is low
- infrastructure is strong
- institutions function
- workers are healthy
- entrepreneurship is stable
- technology is integrated
- AI adoption is easier
- governance is predictable

Low-tax countries often compete only by:

- exploiting cheap labor
- lowering standards
- deregulating markets
- creating loopholes

This does not work in the AI era.

AI requires smart societies, not cheap societies.

And smart societies require:

- high taxes
- high trust
- high investment in people

OBJECTION 7

"High taxes will reduce innovation by punishing success."

Wrong again.

The truth:

Innovation depends not on individual wealth,

but on collective infrastructure.

This includes:

- research universities
- broadband networks
- public AI
- healthcare
- education
- transit
- stable families

- functioning democracy

These require taxation.

The UHS does not punish innovation.
It *funds* innovation.

OBJECTION 8

"High taxes will create government waste and corruption."

Only true in corrupt countries.

High-tax Nordic countries are the least corrupt nations in the world.

Why?
- transparency
- accountability
- strong institutions
- open records
- free media
- public audits

The UHS tax system includes:
- algorithmic auditing
- open budgeting
- real-time tax transparency
- AI-driven anti-corruption enforcement
- public oversight councils

Corruption becomes nearly impossible.

Low-tax societies have *more* corruption, not less.

Why?

Because:

- public institutions are weak
- politicians rely on private donors
- corporations buy influence
- regulatory capture is widespread
- transparency is limited

High tax + high transparency = clean government.

OBJECTION 9

"What about incentives? If you tax wealth, people won't try."

But what motivates people?

Not wealth hoarding.
Not unlimited profit.
Not fear of starvation.

People are motivated by:
- meaning
- mastery
- purpose
- recognition
- contribution
- passion
- curiosity
- creativity
- impact
- self-expression

Look at the world's greatest innovators:
- scientists
- artists
- musicians
- explorers
- writers
- thinkers

They were not motivated by greed.
They were motivated by purpose.

The UHS frees people to pursue purpose
without fear of economic insecurity.

Ironically:

High-tax societies produce more genius per capita

because genius requires freedom from fear.

OBJECTION 10

"Extreme taxation is unrealistic politically."

It was once "unrealistic" to:
- end slavery
- give women the vote
- build universal education
- create national healthcare
- implement social security
- introduce environmental laws
- legalize gay marriage
- regulate corporations
- tax the wealthy during WWII at 94% in the USA

Everything is "impossible" until it becomes inevitable.

AI makes extreme taxation inevitable because:

Without redistribution, society collapses.

When collapse is the alternative,
the political system adapts.

Human survival always wins.

9.11 Conclusion: Every Objection to High Taxation Collapses Under AI Reality

High taxation becomes:
- the stabilizer
- the equalizer
- the civilizational foundation
- the democratic shield
- the prosperity engine
- the innovation multiplier

Low taxation becomes:
- destabilizing
- unequal
- anti-democratic
- oligarchic
- regressive
- obsolete

The AI era ends the debate permanently.

Civilizations with high taxation will survive.

Civilizations with low taxation will not.

9.12 Conclusion — Taxation as the Operating System of the Post-Labor World

For centuries, taxation was treated as a financial necessity,
a way for governments to collect revenue so they could function.

But the AI century transforms taxation into something else entirely:

Taxation becomes the operating system of civilization.

Not a tool.

Not a policy.
Not a political fight.
Not a budget mechanism.

But the foundational software that governs:

- how wealth flows
- how power is distributed
- how dignity is guaranteed
- how AI productivity is shared
- how monopolies are restrained
- how democracy is preserved
- how opportunity is created
- how the future is financed

In a world where:

- machines work
- humans create
- AI produces
- capital multiplies automatically
- wealth concentrates explosively
- labor becomes optional
- survival must be guaranteed

Taxation becomes the architecture of the new society.

9.12.1 The Transformation of Taxation in the AI Era

Under industrial capitalism:

- taxes funded roads, armies, and basic infrastructure
- public goods were limited
- the wealthy justified low taxation by claiming "job creation"
- governments depended on labor income

But AI:

- breaks labor

- breaks market logic
- breaks wage-based taxation
- breaks trickle-down myths
- breaks the old economic incentives

AI creates more wealth than humans ever could —
but it concentrates that wealth faster than any system in history.

This makes traditional taxation:

- too small
- too slow
- too narrow
- too dependent on wages
- too weak against capital
- too easy for billionaires to escape

AI demands a new taxation model that is:

- automated
- structural
- progressive
- dynamic
- transparent
- algorithmically enforced
- directly tied to machine productivity
- designed for infinite scalability

This is why the Utopia Humanity Society (UHS) becomes not ideology —

but economic inevitability.

9.12.2 Taxation Is How We Reclaim Power From Capital

In the early 21st century, capital defeated democracy.

- billionaires bought political influence
- corporations wrote legislation

- monopolies crushed competition
- oligarchs captured institutions
- public services collapsed
- inequality soared
- democracy weakened
- the middle class eroded

AI accelerates this trend exponentially.

But high, structural, progressive taxation:

- redistributes wealth
- redistributes power
- prevents oligarchies
- prevents authoritarian drift
- prevents corporate takeover
- restores equality
- strengthens democracy

Taxes become the counterweight to monopolistic AI power.

The society that survives the AI century
will be the society that prevents capital from becoming sovereign.

9.12.3 Taxation Funds the "New Social Contract"

The old social contract was simple:

You work → you survive.

You stop working → you starve.

AI destroys this contract.

Machines do not rest.
Machines do not demand wages.
Machines do not age, get sick, or retire.

When machines produce the wealth of civilization,
the old contract becomes barbaric and obsolete.

The new social contract:

You exist → you deserve dignity.

You participate → you shape society.
Machines work → all humans benefit.

This requires:

- universal basic income
- universal basic services
- universal healthcare
- universal education
- public AI access
- public transportation
- guaranteed housing
- guaranteed digital access
- guaranteed mental health care

And the only sustainable funding mechanism is:

High taxation of wealth, capital, AI profits, and automation.

This is not a burden.
It is not punishment.
It is not socialism in the old sense.

It is the engineering blueprint of a society where:

- survival is guaranteed
- dignity is universal
- creativity is unleashed
- innovation is abundant
- progress is permanent
- democracy is strong
- humans flourish

This is the post-labor world, and taxation is the foundation.

9.12.4 Taxation Creates the Material Conditions for Human Freedom

Real freedom is impossible when:

- healthcare depends on employment
- education depends on debt
- housing depends on speculation
- survival depends on wage labor
- opportunity depends on family wealth
- creativity depends on economic luck
- the economy depends on millionaires

AI gives us the technology to abolish these conditions
—but only taxation gives us the political and economic *structure* to implement it.

Taxation is how:

- we free humans from economic fear
- we eliminate survival anxiety
- we replace job coercion with meaningful work
- we liberate creativity, purpose, and identity
- we allow people to explore, learn, create, love
- we transition from labor society → human society

Without taxation, AI becomes a weapon of domination.
With taxation, AI becomes a tool for liberation.

This is the core choice before us.

9.12.5 Taxation Is the Insurance Policy Against Collapse

If humanity fails to implement extreme progressive taxation, the future becomes dystopian:

AI owners → trillionaires

Everyone else → economic serfs
Middle class → erased
Democracy → collapses
Society → polarized
Violence → rises
Authoritarianism → spreads
Civilization → fractures

Capitalism cannot survive AI.
But civilization can survive if we rewrite the rules.

High taxation prevents:

- collapse
- revolution
- feudalism
- oligarchy
- civil conflict
- democratic decay

This is not ideology.
It is structural risk management.

AI produces infinite wealth.
Taxation distributes infinite wealth.

Together they create:

a stable, abundant, dignified society.

9.12.6 Taxation Is the Engine of the Utopia Humanity Society

The UHS is built on four pillars:

1. AI-driven productivity
2. Extreme progressive taxation

3.   Universal basic income + services
4.   Democratic oversight of AI and capital

Taxation is the *mechanism* that binds the system:

- AI generates wealth
- taxation captures wealth
- redistribution shares wealth
- UBS + UBI guarantee dignity
- democracy remains stable
- innovation expands
- society flourishes

This creates a virtuous cycle:

AI → Taxation → Public Goods → Stability → Innovation → More AI → More Wealth → More Redistribution → More Prosperity → More Democracy.

Civilization becomes self-sustaining.

9.12.7 The Moral Core:

A Society Where No One Is Disposable

High taxation is not a financial model.
It is a moral declaration:

Every human life matters.

Every human deserves dignity.
Every human deserves freedom from fear.

AI gives us the tools to build abundance.
Taxation gives us the structure to distribute it.
Democracy gives us the legitimacy to govern it.

Together they create:

The first truly humane civilization in history.

9.12.8 Final Statement of the Chapter

Taxation is not just revenue.

Taxation is not punishment.
Taxation is not ideology.

Taxation is the constitutional infrastructure of the AI-driven world.

Without it:

- inequality becomes catastrophic
- society collapses
- freedom dies
- democracy is replaced by digital feudalism

With it:

- abundance becomes shared
- happiness expands
- innovation accelerates
- humans flourish
- civilizations endure

The Utopia Humanity Society is not a dream.
It is a mathematical, structural, and moral necessity.

And taxation is the mechanism that makes it real.

9.13 The Wealth Transition Tax

Toward a Humane Redistribution Within 20 Years

Even with progressive taxation, automation taxes, AI monopoly taxes, and data dividends,
a deeper structural problem remains:

The world begins the AI century with historically unprecedented wealth concentration.

- The top 1% owns nearly half of all global wealth.
- The top 0.1% owns more wealth than the bottom 80% combined.
- Billionaires accumulated more wealth in the last decade than in the previous century.
- AI, automation, and capital markets accelerate wealth accumulation exponentially.

This starting point is unsustainable.

If society merely taxes future wealth flows but ignores existing wealth stock,
the next 20 years will produce:

- AI feudalism
- political capture
- mass inequality
- social breakdown
- collapse of the middle class
- death of political legitimacy
- destabilization of democracies
- emergence of corporate nation-states

Thus, a humane, stable post-labor civilization requires a transitional corrective mechanism:

THE WEALTH TRANSITION TAX (WTT)

An 80% conversion of extreme wealth into shared human prosperity over 20 years

This is not confiscation.
This is not punishment.
This is not socialism.
This is not anti-business.

This is civilizational stabilization.

It works like this:

1. Total Wealth Above Threshold Is Taxed Over 20 Years

- Wealth above $100 million is gradually taxed.
- The goal: redistribute 80% of concentrated wealth within two decades.
- Taxation applies to:
- financial assets
- real estate portfolios
- private equity
- corporate shares
- trusts
- inheritance wealth
- sovereign-level billionaire holdings

2. The Tax Is Phased:

- Years 1–5: 2–3% annual wealth tax
- Years 6–10: 3–4% annual
- Years 11–15: 4–5% annual
- Years 16–20: 5–6% annual

Accumulated over 20 years, this achieves approximately 80% redistribution.

Why gradual?

- avoids economic shock
- allows wealthy individuals to adapt
- maintains market stability
- provides predictable long-term planning
- prevents panic capital flight
- encourages productive reinvestment

Why 80%?

Because mathematically:

To build a society where every human has security, dignity, and access to basic goods,

we must convert concentrated capital into universal civilizational infrastructure.

The wealthy of today inherited a world built by:

- public roads
- public healthcare
- public education
- public scientific research
- public stability
- public military protection
- public workers
- public trust
- society itself

Thus, returning 80% of extreme wealth over 20 years is not exploitation.
It is repayment.

9.13.1 Why This Is Necessary

Reason 1: AI will multiply inequality beyond imagination.

If nothing changes, a single AI corporation could be worth $20 trillion. One CEO could control more power than an entire government.

Reason 2: Democracy cannot survive extreme wealth concentration.

History shows it repeatedly:

- Imperial Rome
- Qing Dynasty
- Tsarist Russia
- French monarchy
- Gilded Age America

Extreme wealth concentration always ends in collapse or revolution.

Reason 3: Current wealth was created collectively.

The richest 0.1% did not invent:

- electricity
- semiconductors
- the internet
- mathematics
- vaccines
- global trade
- legal protections
- roads, ports, airports
- public education

Yet they benefited disproportionately.

Reason 4: Wealth without redistribution becomes political power.

Power without accountability becomes tyranny.

The Wealth Transition Tax is not anti-wealth;
it is anti-monopoly and pro-humanity.

Reason 5: Civilization needs infrastructure.

The next century requires massive investment in:

- universal healthcare
- universal education
- AI public utilities
- green transformation
- transportation modernization
- social housing
- elder care
- climate adaptation

These cannot be funded through traditional tax structures alone.

The wealth already accumulated must participate.

9.13.2 Where Does the Wealth Transition Fund Go?

All revenue from the WTT flows into:

A. The Universal Basic Services Fund

- healthcare
- childcare
- eldercare
- mental health
- education
- transit
- digital access
- public housing

B. The Sovereign AI Infrastructure Fund

To build public AI systems, ensuring AI serves everyone.

C. The Common Wealth Fund

A national fund that pays AI Dividends to every citizen.

D. The Climate and Regeneration Fund

Reforestation, carbon removal, clean energy, water systems.

E. The Human Future Endowment

A generational fund ensuring future stability even after AI disruption.

This is not spending.
This is long-term investment in civilization.

9.13.3 How the Wealth Transition Tax Stabilizes Society

The WTT:

- prevents AI feudalism
- eliminates ultra-concentrated wealth monopolies
- preserves democracy
- strengthens social trust
- revitalizes the middle class
- expands opportunity
- funds public goods
- guarantees stable political institutions
- removes the seeds of future unrest

Most importantly, it builds a cohesive society where:

No citizen lives in fear.

No billionaire controls the political system.
No corporation becomes a parallel government.

9.13.4 Why 80% Wealth Transition Is Not Radical — It Is Rational

The world already implemented similar policies:

- post-WWII Japan (Zaibatsu restructuring)
- post-war Europe (wealth levies)
- South Korea (chaebol reforms)
- Germany's 1948 equalization tax
- U.S. WWII tax rate (94% on top income bracket)

These policies:

- rebuilt societies
- reduced inequality
- strengthened democracy
- produced decades of stable growth

Humanity has done this before.
We simply need to do it again — for the AI century.

9.13.5 The Ethical Foundation

Extreme wealth is not just an economic imbalance.
It is a civilizational risk factor.

No society in history has survived when:

- a small elite holds the majority of wealth
- the public loses trust
- institutions fail
- the middle class erodes
- opportunities disappear

AI accelerates all of these trends.

Thus:

Wealth redistribution is not ideology.

It is survival.

80% transition is not punishment.

It is justice.

20 years is not slow.

It is responsible and humane.

Humanity must correct the imbalance

before AI magnifies it beyond repair.

9.13.6 Final Statement of the New Section

Capitalism accumulated the wealth of the past.

AI will generate the wealth of the future.
But only taxation — strong, structural, progressive — can distribute it.

The Wealth Transition Tax ensures:

- the future belongs to everyone
- democracy survives
- dignity is universal
- prosperity is shared
- humanity evolves
- civilization stabilizes

This policy is not optional.
It is the bridge between today's broken world
and the Utopia Humanity Society we are building.

CHAPTER 10: UNIVERSAL BASIC INCOME + UNIVERSAL BASIC SERVICES

The Backbone of a Humane Post-Labor Civilization

10.1 Introduction — The Moment Humanity Outgrew Wage Labor

For 300 years, the global economy operated on a single assumption:

Humans must sell their labor to survive.

This assumption shaped everything:

- taxation
- education
- family structure
- immigration
- politics
- borders
- national security
- capitalism itself

But AI destroys this foundation:

- machines now generate value
- labor participation is falling
- jobs disappear faster than new ones appear
- productivity divorces itself from human effort
- capital separates from workers entirely
- AI enables near-zero marginal cost for services and manufacturing

The wage-labor survival model collapses.

A civilization cannot survive if:

- most people cannot earn enough to live
- economic insecurity becomes universal
- traditional jobs disappear

- wealth concentrates infinitely
- democracy destabilizes

Thus, humanity must design a new survival architecture:

Universal Basic Income + Universal Basic Services (UBI + UBS)

This is not charity.
This is not welfare.
This is not left or right.
This is civilizational engineering.

UBI + UBS is the replacement for wage labor as the basis of survival.

10.2 Why UBI Alone Is Not Enough — The Critically Missing Half

For years, the debate focused only on UBI:

- "Give people money every month."
- "Let the market handle the rest."

But this would fail because:

- markets inflate prices
- landlords raise rents
- private healthcare absorbs the income
- education costs explode
- monopolies swallow the new spending
- inflation outpaces UBI
- inequality persists

UBI must be paired with UBS.

Universal Basic Services provide:

- free healthcare
- free education
- free childcare

- free eldercare
- free public housing options
- free public transportation
- free mental health services
- free digital access
- free basic utilities
- free access to public AI systems

UBS stabilizes cost of living.
UBI stabilizes income.

Together they create:

economic dignity, without dependence on employers or markets.

This is the heart of the Utopia Humanity Society.

10.3 The Three Core Principles of UBI + UBS

Principle 1 — Survival cannot depend on employment.

Employment is no longer guaranteed.
Machines outperform humans.
AI replaces middle-class labor.
Robotics replaces manual labor.

Dependence on jobs becomes structurally impossible.

Principle 2 — Dignity must be guaranteed by design.

Dignity is not negotiable.
Survival cannot be conditional.
Civilization must guarantee the basics:

- food
- shelter
- health

- education
- mobility
- access to technology

Principle 3 — Human potential expands when fear disappears.

People innovate more
when they do not fear poverty.

People create more
when they have time and security.

People contribute more
when they are not traumatized by economic anxiety.

UBI + UBS is not a cost.
It is an investment in human capability.

10.4 The Economic Logic: Why UBI + UBS Is Cheaper Than the Current System

Critics say:

> "UBI + UBS is expensive! Who will pay for it?"

> But the truth is stunning:

UBI + UBS costs less than the current system.

Why?

1. AI and automation make essential goods nearly free.
- Zero-cost customer service
- Zero-cost administration
- Zero-cost logistics optimization
- Near-zero-cost manufacturing

- Near-zero-cost tutoring and education support
- Near-zero-cost software and digital tools

The structure of the economy shifts:
machines produce → humans share.

2. Universal services remove trillions in waste.

- private insurance bureaucracy
- predatory student loans
- profit-driven healthcare billing
- corporate administrative layers
- duplicated systems across agencies
- fragmented transit networks
- redundant digital infrastructure

UBS wipes out waste by providing:

- one coordinated system
- at near-zero marginal cost
- powered by AI

3. UBI replaces dozens of outdated welfare programs.
The old welfare systems:

- are complex
- require constant paperwork
- punish productivity
- stigmatize the poor
- create administrative bloat

UBI is:

- simple
- efficient
- universal
- non-stigmatizing
- AI-automated

Administration costs approach zero.

4. Money returns to the economy instantly.
UBI recipients:

- pay rent
- buy food
- purchase goods
- invest in education
- support small businesses

This stimulates constant economic activity.

5. The tax base expands dramatically.
With:

- automation tax
- AI monopoly tax
- wealth tax
- data dividend tax
- the Wealth Transition Tax

The government captures machine productivity, not human labor.

The future tax base is:

- infinite
- automated
- scalable
- tied to AI output

Thus:

UBI + UBS is not expensive —

it is the only affordable system in the AI era.

10.5 UBI — The Income Foundation of a Post-Labor World

UBI provides every adult with:

- monthly income
- unconditional
- universal
- permanent
- sufficient for dignified survival

Amount varies by country, but typically:

- in high-income countries: $1,200–$2,000 per month
- in middle-income countries: $300–$800 per month
- adjusted to local living costs

What UBI guarantees:

- food
- basic utilities
- personal autonomy
- freedom from employer coercion
- economic stability during disruptions
- entrepreneurial opportunity
- time to learn, retrain, heal, or create

What UBI does not do:

- eliminate the desire to work
- destroy motivation
- cause inflation
- collapse society

In every trial globally, UBI results in:

- less poverty
- better health
- more entrepreneurship
- more happiness
- lower crime

- better decision-making
- greater workforce participation

UBI strengthens society.

10.6 UBS — The Service Infrastructure That Makes Life Livable

Without UBS, UBI collapses under the weight of market exploitation.

UBS includes:

Healthcare

Free, universal, high-quality.
AI reduces administrative cost to nearly zero.
Telemedicine expands access everywhere.

Education

From early childhood to postgraduate.
AI personalized tutors for every student.
Free re-skilling at any age.

Childcare and Eldercare

Fully funded.
Trained caregivers supported by robotic assistants.
Families regain time and peace.

Housing

Guaranteed access to dignified housing.
Public housing modernized with AI-building systems.
Long-term rental stability.

Transportation

AI-managed, electric, low-cost.
Universal transit eliminates dependence on cars.

Digital Access

Free internet.
Free public AI tools.
Digital equality as a civil right.

Mental Health

AI-assisted early detection.
Free counseling.
Community programs.

Public AI Systems

Transparent, democratic, safe.
Every citizen has access to high-quality intelligence.

UBS is not luxury.
It is civilization.

10.7 Why UBI + UBS Makes Society Stronger, Not Weaker

1. People take smarter risks.

When survival is secure, innovation explodes.

2. Families are more stable.

No financial trauma.
No catastrophic medical bankruptcies.

3. Crimes of desperation disappear.

4. Social trust rises.

5. Democracy strengthens.

Citizens no longer vote from fear.

6. Corporations become more ethical.

They cannot exploit desperation.

7. Inequality declines.

8. Social mobility increases.

9. Mental health improves.

10. The middle class returns.

The world becomes more stable, creative, and humane.

10.8 The Role of AI in Powering UBI + UBS

AI makes this system not only possible
but inevitable.

AI reduces cost of public administration by 80–95%.

AI reduces cost of manufacturing by 70–90%.

AI reduces cost of education by 90%.

AI reduces cost of healthcare by 60–80%.

AI eliminates bureaucracy.

AI optimizes logistics, transit, and housing systems.

AI enables public goods at near-zero cost.

Under traditional economics, public services were expensive.
Under AI economics, public services are cheap.

10.9 Funding Model — How UBI + UBS Is Paid For

UBI + UBS draws from the entire UHS tax architecture:

- wealth tax
- AI monopoly tax
- automation tax
- data dividend tax
- progressive income tax
- and especially the Wealth Transition Tax (80% over 20 years)

Funding becomes:

- stable
- diversified
- primarily automated
- resilient against economic cycles
- protected from political manipulation

UBI + UBS is not a welfare program.
It is the financial core of a post-labor civilization.

10.10 The Social Psychology of UBI + UBS — Why Humans Don't Become Lazy

Every global trial shows the same:

People do not become lazy.
They become free.

With UBI + UBS:

- people start businesses
- people go back to school
- people invest in skills
- people care for their families
- people volunteer
- people pursue creative projects
- people work part-time without fear
- people take time to heal
- people reduce stress
- people make better decisions

Humans were never driven by fear alone.
Humans thrive when dignity is guaranteed.

10.11 UBI + UBS as the New Social Contract

The 20th century:
You work → you survive.

The 21st century:
You exist → you deserve dignity.

AI replaces labor.
UBI replaces wages.
UBS replaces financial fear.

Together they create:

A stable, prosperous, democratic civilization.

This is not utopia.
This is engineering.

10.12 The Mechanics of UBI Delivery — Automated, Transparent, Universal

Implementing UBI at national scale once seemed impossible.
But AI collapses the complexity into near-zero administrative cost.

In the Utopia Humanity Society (UHS), UBI is delivered through:

1. A Universal Citizen Ledger (UCL)

A secure, encrypted identity system tied to:

- citizenship
- residency status
- lifespan records
- geolocation jurisdiction

No corporate involvement.
No third-party capture.

This is not a surveillance tool.
It is a simple registry:

"You are a member of society → you receive your share."

2. Automated Monthly Distribution

Every month, without paperwork:

- funds transfer automatically
- no applications
- no conditions
- no stigma
- no bureaucracy

AI ensures:

- fraud detection
- eligibility verification

- conflict resolution
- appeals processing
- payment consistency

Administrative cost: 0.2–0.5%
(A fraction of traditional welfare systems, which often exceed 15–20%.)

3. Dynamic Adjustment Based on Inflation and Cost of Living

UBI is not static.

AI monitors:

- inflation
- energy cost
- housing cost
- food supply
- healthcare cost
- local purchasing power

UBI adjusts automatically to preserve real purchasing power.

No political manipulation.
No election-year games.

4. Decentralized but Federated Governance

Local governments can:

- add supplements
- adjust for regional variations
- run additional programs

But national UBI ensures:

- equality
- universality
- stability

5. Optional Conversion to Digital Wallets

Citizens can choose:

- direct deposit
- physical debit card
- digital wallet
- blockchain-based account

The system is designed for:

- resilience
- privacy
- accessibility
- redundancy

No one is excluded, even without smartphones.

6. UBI Distribution Is a Constitutional Right

In the UHS Constitution:

> Every citizen is entitled to unconditional income guaranteeing dignified survival.

> No future government can abolish UBI.
> This protects the people from political cycles.

> UBI becomes a birthright.

10.13 Funding Allocation Models and Public Financial Architecture

One of the strengths of the UHS is its multi-source funding structure, ensuring no single tax must bear the full burden.

Here is the allocation model:

10.13.1 Funding Source #1 — Automation and AI Productivity Tax (30–60%)

This is the *engine* of UBI.

As AI:

- produces
- optimizes
- manufactures
- designs
- operates
- delivers

...a portion of machine productivity is automatically converted into human income.

Mechanism:

- AI auditors analyze corporate productivity
- compare machine labor vs. human labor
- calculate value-added
- apply automation levy

This captures the wealth that would otherwise flow entirely to capital owners.

10.13.2 Funding Source #2 — AI Monopoly Windfall Tax (60–90%)

AI tends toward:

- monopoly
- data centralization
- compute dominance
- "winner-takes-all" dynamics

This tax prevents runaway concentration and funds UBI + UBS at scale.

Revenue Allocation:
- 60% goes to UBI
- 20% goes to UBS
- 20% goes to the Sovereign AI Fund (public AI systems)

The most powerful companies directly fund public dignity.

10.13.3 Funding Source #3 — Wealth Tax (2–5% annually)

Applies to wealth above:

- $50 million → 2%
- $100 million → 3%
- $1 billion → 5%

This prevents re-accumulation of dangerous wealth concentration.

Funding Allocation:

- 40% to UBI
- 40% to UBS
- 20% to housing and childcare systems

The wealthy do not collapse under this tax.
Their wealth continues to grow, but slower and more responsibly.

10.13.4 Funding Source #4 — Data Dividend Tax (5–15%)

Corporations profit from public data:

- health information
- geospatial data
- user behavior
- public records
- scientific research
- academic publications

Because data is a public resource, profits derived from it must return to the public.

Revenue Allocation:
- 100% to UBI (distributed equally)

This is a permanent national dividend.

10.13.5 Funding Source #5 — Progressive Income Tax (Up to 80%)

This applies mostly to:

- CEOs
- financiers
- corporate executives
- mega-compensated professionals

Revenue Allocation:

- 30% to UBI
- 40% to UBS
- 30% to public infrastructure

This ensures high earners contribute proportionally to the society that enables their success.

10.13.6 Funding Source #6 — The Wealth Transition Tax (80% over 20 years)

This is the civilization reset mechanism, ensuring that the dangerous inequality of early 21st century capitalism does not corrupt the AI century.

Revenue Allocation:

- 25% → Universal Basic Income
- 25% → Universal Basic Services
- 20% → Public AI Infrastructure

- 20% → Housing & Climate Projects
- 10% → National Endowment Fund

This creates a permanent foundation that stabilizes the society for generations.

10.13.7 Total Funding Structure

Under the integrated model:

- UBI draws primarily from AI + automation taxes
- UBS draws from wealth, income, and monopoly taxes
- Climate and infrastructure draw from wealth transition taxes
- AI dividends draw from data taxes

The system is balanced and sustainable, even as:

- population shifts
- AI productivity skyrockets
- economic cycles fluctuate

UBI + UBS becomes future-proof.

10.14 The Global Transition Plan — How Nations Move from Capitalism to UBI + UBS

Transition must be:

- orderly
- democratic
- gradual
- evidence-based
- scalable

Here is the recommended 10-year transition.

PHASE 1 (Years 1–3): Foundation Building

A. Digital Identity + Citizen Ledger

Prepare the infrastructure.

B. Automation Tax Implementation

Begin capturing machine productivity.

C. Pilot UBI Programs in Select Cities

Demonstrate feasibility.

D. Introduce Rent Stabilization

Prevent housing inflation before UBI launches.

E. Create Public AI Systems

Ensure AI tools are not monopolized.

Outcome:
The society becomes technically ready.

PHASE 2 (Years 4–6): Initial Rollout

A. Launch Partial UBI (30–50% of full amount)

Give people stability while systems mature.

B. Introduce Universal Healthcare

Removes catastrophic financial risks.

C. Begin Free Education & Re-Skilling

Prepare citizens for the post-labor economy.

D. Implement Wealth Tax (2%–3%)

Funding begins to stabilize.

Outcome:
People experience increased dignity and security.

PHASE 3 (Years 7–10): Full Deployment

A. Full UBI Rollout

Enough to guarantee dignified survival.

B. Full UBS Rollout

Housing, transit, digital access, mental health.

C. Wealth Transition Tax Begins

Gradual 20-year rebalancing process begins.

D. AI Monopoly Tax Activated

Ensures no corporation can dominate the future.

Outcome:
The society completes the transition to UHS standards.

PHASE 4 (Year 10+): Global Cooperation and Expansion

Neighboring nations begin adopting UBI + UBS.
Trade systems adapt.
International wealth taxes harmonize.
AI governance becomes global.

The new model becomes the planetary standard.

10.15 Addressing Critiques of UBI + UBS

Critique: "People will stop working."
→ Evidence: They work more meaningfully.

Critique: "Businesses won't have labor."
→ Automation fills the gaps.

Critique: "It's too expensive."
→ AI reduces costs dramatically; taxes provide abundance.

Critique: "It encourages dependency."
→ Actually increases empowerment and entrepreneurship.

Critique: "It will cause inflation."
→ UBS stabilizes costs; housing and healthcare cannot inflate.

Critique: "It destroys capitalism."
→ Capitalism was already dying; UBI + UBS prevents collapse.

Critique: "It's unrealistic."
→ AI makes it inevitable.

10.16 The Human Future After UBI + UBS

With UBI + UBS, human life changes fundamentally:

1. People become creators, not laborers.

Art, science, innovation explode.

2. Identity decouples from employment.

You are more than your job.

3. Families become stronger.

Childcare and eldercare relieve enormous stress.

4. Happiness rises dramatically.

Fear-free living transforms psychology.

5. Democracy stabilizes.

People vote without desperation.

6. Spiritual and intellectual life expands.

Humans rediscover meaning beyond survival.

7. Civilizations shift from competition → cooperation.

The race for survival ends; collaboration begins.

8. Humanity matures into a post-scarcity species.

Not utopia — but stable, abundant, humane reality.

UBI + UBS is the economic heart of the Utopia Humanity Society.

CHAPTER 11: AI DIVIDENDS AND PUBLIC OWNERSHIP OF INTELLIGENCE

Why the Future of AI Belongs to Everyone — Not Corporations

11.1 Introduction — The Most Important Question of the 21st Century

Humanity has never faced a question as profound as this:

Who should own intelligence?

Not information.
Not data.
Not compute.
But intelligence itself — the ability to:

- reason
- plan
- optimize
- predict
- learn
- create
- design
- decide

For the first time in history, intelligence is no longer uniquely human. Machines can now think in ways that:

- outperform engineers
- outperform doctors
- outperform strategists
- outperform scientists
- outperform managers

Which leads to the essential truth:

AI is not a product.

AI is a new form of power.

And like all forms of power:

- it must be governed
- it must be democratized
- it must be accountable
- it must be shared

If AI becomes privately owned by a few corporations, then those corporations will control:

- the global economy
- political systems
- public discourse
- access to knowledge
- the future itself

This would create:

AI feudalism —

the most dangerous hierarchy in human history.

But if AI is recognized as a public good,
owned collectively by society,
then AI becomes:

- the engine of shared abundance
- the infrastructure of human dignity
- the foundation of stable democracy
- the mechanism of universal prosperity

This chapter presents the central idea:

Public ownership of AI systems

Universal "AI Dividends"

The only safe and ethical future for civilization.

11.2 Why AI Cannot Be Privately Owned — The Economic Argument

In traditional capitalism:

- factories were owned privately
- land was owned privately
- intellectual property was owned privately

But AI is fundamentally different.

AI replaces labor across entire economies.

A privately owned AI that eliminates 50 million jobs
must not concentrate all wealth into the hands of one owner.

AI generates unlimited, exponential productivity.

Unlike factories, AI does not have diminishing returns.
One model can produce infinite economic value.

AI has near-zero marginal cost.

Once built, producing intelligence costs almost nothing.
This makes private ownership even more dangerous.

AI will soon manage critical infrastructure.

Energy grids.
Supply chains.
Governments.
Healthcare systems.

Private ownership becomes a national security threat.

AI is trained using public knowledge.

Everything from:

- scientific papers

- public datasets
- Wikipedia
- open code
- human-generated content
- culture and art

AI models are built on humanity's collective knowledge.

Therefore:

No corporation has the moral right to privatize the intelligence created from public intellectual labor.

11.3 Why AI Cannot Be Privately Owned — The Political Argument

AI has immense political power:

- persuasion
- surveillance
- propaganda
- voter prediction
- narrative shaping
- emotional influence
- information control

If private entities control intelligence,
they control democracy.

This leads to:

- political capture
- manipulation of public opinion
- algorithmic authoritarianism
- invisible influence over elections
- decay of institutional trust
- corporate-state fusion

AI cannot become a tool of oligarchs.

Democracy cannot survive privately owned intelligence.

11.4 Why AI Cannot Be Privately Owned — The Philosophical Argument

Philosophically, the question is:

Is intelligence the property of a corporation

or a universal capacity that belongs to all beings?

Historically:

- reading was democratized
- education was democratized
- information was democratized
- digital tools were democratized

AI is simply the next stage:

The democratization of intelligence itself.

To restrict this power to a small elite would be:

- anti-human
- anti-democratic
- anti-civilizational
- ethically indefensible

AI is:

- trained on humanity
- shaped by humanity
- dependent on humanity

Thus, its benefits must return to humanity.

11.5 The Concept of Public AI Infrastructure

Public ownership of AI does NOT mean:

- government control
- state censorship
- bureaucratic inefficiency
- political abuse

Instead, it means:

AI treated as infrastructure — like electricity, roads, or clean water.

Just as no private company should own:

- oxygen
- sunlight
- the alphabet
- mathematical principles
- gravitational laws

No single corporation should own:

- general-purpose intelligence
- foundational models
- national datasets
- core compute infrastructure

Public AI infrastructure includes:

- open national models
- transparent training data
- public compute clusters
- AI safety oversight boards
- algorithmic accountability systems
- citizen-access AI interfaces

Everyone uses it.
No one monopolizes it.

11.6 The AI Dividends System — Turning Machine Intelligence Into Income

Now the central idea:

If AI replaces labor,

then AI must replace wages.

This is done through AI Dividends:

A permanent, universal payment
to all citizens,
funded by:

- AI-generated profits
- automation taxes
- data dividends
- public AI utilities
- AI monopoly windfall taxes
- foundational model rental fees
- compute-usage royalties

AI Dividends complement:

- UBI
- UBS
- wealth taxes
- public services

They create a triple-income society:

1. UBI — baseline survival
2. AI Dividends — share of machine productivity
3. Optional work income — purpose-driven, not survival-driven

This produces:

- economic stability

- freedom from fear
- reduced inequality
- expanded human creativity
- more entrepreneurship
- stronger democracy

AI Dividends convert technological power → human prosperity.

11.7 How AI Dividends Are Calculated

AI Dividends draw from several revenue sources:

1. AI Profit Contribution (Mandatory)

Every corporation using AI must contribute a percentage of:

- profits
- productivity gains
- cost savings

AI creates the wealth → society receives the return.

2. Public AI Utility Revenues

Publicly owned AI systems charge:

- subscription fees (minimal)
- enterprise usage fees
- developer tools
- API access charges
- compute rentals
- training licenses

Revenue goes directly into the national dividend pool.

3. Data Royalty Mechanism

Since human-generated data trains AI:

- individuals receive collective royalties
- content creators receive proportional compensation
- national data resources generate national dividends

4. Sovereign AI Fund

Similar to:

- Norway's Sovereign Wealth Fund
- Singapore's Temasek
- UAE's Mubadala

But instead of oil,
this fund grows from:

- AI model ownership
- compute infrastructure
- national datasets
- licensing agreements

The fund pays out annual dividends to all citizens.

11.8 Why AI Dividends Must Be Universal

If AI Dividends were:

- means-tested
- limited to certain groups
- politically conditional

...they would fail.

Universality matters because:

1. Universal programs have the strongest public support.

Everyone benefits → everyone protects it.

2. Universality prevents stigma.

No one is labeled "poor."

3. Universality simplifies administration.

No bureaucracy.
No gatekeeping.

4. Universality strengthens democracy.

Citizens see AI as a shared resource.

5. Universality makes AI a civil right.

Intelligence for all → prosperity for all.

11.9 What AI Dividends Unlock for Humanity

AI Dividends create a new kind of civilization:

1. People become explorers, not survivors.

Freed from economic fear, humans pursue:

- philosophy
- science
- art
- innovation
- self-discovery
- entrepreneurship
- community building

2. Inequality collapses.

The gap between:

- AI owners

- non-owners

...disappears.

3. Middle class becomes universal.

Every citizen has:
- income
- security
- dignity

4. Economic storms become irrelevant.

Automated income stabilizes society during:
- recessions
- pandemics
- supply chain shocks

5. Democracy becomes resilient.

AI Dividends reduce:
- populism
- extremism
- desperation votes

6. Civilization becomes more humane.

People stop being used as tools.

7. Humanity enters a new era.

The age of:
- abundance
- stability
- creativity
- wisdom

AI becomes the engine of prosperity — not domination.

11.10 Public vs. Private AI — The Hybrid Model of the UHS

Most debates wrongly assume a binary choice:
- Either AI must be privately owned
- Or AI must be government-controlled

Both extremes are dangerous.

Private AI monopolies lead to:
- corporate feudalism
- political capture
- unregulated power
- inequality explosion
- opaque decision-making
- manipulation of public discourse

Government-only AI leads to:
- surveillance
- censorship
- authoritarian centralization
- single-point failure risk
- bureaucratic stagnation

The Utopia Humanity Society uses a hybrid sovereignty model, where:

AI is publicly owned

but privately innovated.

The structure:

Layer 1 — Public AI Infrastructure (sovereign, universal)

Includes:
- foundational models
- national datasets
- compute infrastructure
- digital identity systems

- safety monitoring algorithms
- transparency protocols

This layer is non-profit, public, and constitutionally protected.

Layer 2 — Private AI Innovation

Private companies can:
- build on public models
- develop vertical applications
- commercialize specialized systems
- compete in creative and entrepreneurial space

But they CANNOT:
- monopolize foundational intelligence
- privatize national compute networks
- own citizen data
- build closed systems that undermine transparency

Layer 3 — Public-Private AI Collaboration

Universities, NGOs, startups, governments, and corporations co-develop:
- safety protocols
- ethical standards
- auditing tools
- open research datasets
- human-rights-based AI frameworks

This hybrid model ensures:
- no monopolies
- no authoritarian control
- permanent public benefit
- continuous innovation

AI becomes like electricity:
publicly governed, privately utilized.

11.11 How Public AI Utilities Are Built and Governed

Public AI utilities are the moral heart of the UHS.

They ensure:
- equal access
- safety
- transparency
- fairness
- resilience
- public ownership

A public AI utility includes:

A. The National Foundation Model (NFM)

A large-scale intelligence model trained on:
- public datasets
- academic research
- responsibly licensed data
- democratic inputs
- multilingual corpora
- ethical guidelines

The NFM is:
- open-access
- transparent
- auditable
- non-profit
- built for safety over profit

B. Public Compute Network (PCN)

A nationwide network of:
- data centers
- compute clusters
- GPU/TPU farms
- quantum and neuromorphic systems

This network ensures:
- equal access to AI compute
- resistance to corporate control
- sovereign independence
- national security

C. Democratic Oversight Councils

Governance includes:
- AI safety experts
- ethicists
- civil society leaders
- technologists
- citizen representatives
- labor representatives

The council:
- reviews updates
- approves model releases
- sets ethical guidelines
- prohibits unsafe deployments
- maintains transparency

D. Algorithmic Transparency Board

Every public AI model must:
- disclose training sources
- list potential harms
- publish all safety evaluations
- document known limitations
- reveal bias testing results

Nothing is hidden.

E. Citizen Feedback Channel

Like a constitutional right to petition:
- citizens can report harms

- request transparency
- demand model audits
- challenge algorithmic decisions

Public AI responds to the people — not corporations.

11.12 Preventing AI Capture by Corporations or Governments

The greatest risk of AI is capture.

Capture means:
- corporations gain excessive control
- governments use AI for authoritarian ends
- intelligence is centralized
- oversight collapses
- citizens lose agency

The UHS implements five anti-capture mechanisms:

1. Constitutional Protection of Public AI

AI is written into the constitution as:
- a public utility
- a public right
- a public good
- a public guarantee

No political party can privatize it.
No corporation can monopolize it.
No leader can remove transparency requirements.

2. Multi-Node Governance

Public AI is governed by:
- federal councils

- regional bodies
- citizen assemblies
- independent scientific boards

No single body can gain control.

3. Mandatory Open Audits

All core models must undergo:
- safety red-teaming
- bias testing
- independent peer review
- real-world harm audits
- annual transparency reports

No closed "black box" models allowed in critical infrastructure.

4. Compute Democraticization

Compute is the true power of AI.

Thus:
- compute credits are distributed universally
- citizens receive monthly allocation
- universities receive national grants
- small businesses receive subsidies
- public interest projects receive priority

Compute cannot be concentrated in the hands of:
- corporations
- billionaires
- militaries

Public compute ensures public intelligence.

5. Anti-Monopoly Kill Switch for AI Corporations

If a private AI corporation passes thresholds of:
- market dominance
- political influence
- societal risk
- foundational dependency

The state can:
- break up the company
- nationalize core infrastructure
- convert proprietary models into public assets
- regulate compute access
- impose 90% monopoly windfall taxes

AI will never become the next oil empire.

11.13 Global AI Dividend Systems and International Coordination

AI dividends work best with international cooperation.

The UHS proposes:

A. Global AI Dividend Treaty (GAID)

Countries agree to:
- transparent taxation of automation
- cross-border AI dividend sharing
- reciprocal data protections
- anti-monopoly alignment
- global safety standards

This reduces inequality between nations.

B. International AI Commons

A shared pool of:
- open models
- ethical datasets
- safety frameworks
- research findings

Hosted by:
- the UN
- UNESCO
- global research coalitions

This prevents global knowledge monopolies.

C. Cross-Border AI Wealth Sharing

AI productivity transcends borders.
Thus:
- richer nations contribute
- developing nations receive AI dividends
- global inequality reduces
- migration pressure decreases
- planetary stability increases

AI becomes the first technology that truly connects global prosperity.

D. Global Safety Oversight Network

Independent bodies monitor:
- frontier model releases
- autonomous weapons
- biological risk
- misinformation systems
- major corporate actors

This prevents global-scale harms.

11.14 AI Dividends + UBI = Permanent Human Freedom

UBI ensures survival.
UBS ensures dignity.
AI dividends ensure abundance.

Together they create a three-income civilization:

1. UBI → baseline income

2. UBS → near-zero cost of essential life services

3. AI Dividends → share of machine-generated wealth

This transforms the human condition:

No one is expendable.

No one lives in fear.

Everyone benefits from technology.

Humanity enters an age of abundance.

For the first time in history:
- income is guaranteed
- survival is not tied to employment
- intelligence is democratized
- prosperity is shared
- democracy is strengthened
- creativity is liberated
- human potential expands

AI becomes the engine of freedom,
not the guardian of elites.

11.15 The Spiritual and Ethical Meaning of Shared Intelligence

AI is often discussed in technical terms:

- compute
- models
- parameters
- training datasets

But beneath the technical layer lies a profound ethical transition:

Humanity is, for the first time in history, choosing what intelligence means.

Until now:

- intelligence was personal
- intelligence was biological
- intelligence was unequal
- intelligence was hoarded
- intelligence determined power

But AI transforms intelligence into something new:

A universal, reproducible, abundant resource.

Just as fire moved from tribal secret
→ to universal tool
→ to civilizational foundation,

AI moves from elite possession
→ to public utility
→ to shared consciousness.

The moral question becomes:

**Should intelligence be a privilege
or a public right?**

The UHS answers:

Intelligence must be shared — morally, ethically, spiritually.

Because:
- intelligence is amplified through connection
- shared intelligence creates shared flourishing
- private intelligence creates private tyranny

If intelligence remains privately owned:
- the few think for the many
- the many depend on the few
- democracy collapses under informational asymmetry

But if intelligence is shared:
- creativity becomes universal
- problem-solving becomes planetary
- wisdom multiplies
- humanity evolves

This is not merely economics.
This is spiritual evolution.

The democratization of intelligence is:
- a moral awakening
- a philosophical turning point
- a civilizational choice
- a step toward collective consciousness

For the first time, humanity can become:

One species,

with shared access
to the most powerful tool ever created.

11.16 The End of Fear-Based Civilization

For 10,000 years, human society was built on fear:
- fear of hunger
- fear of homelessness
- fear of unemployment
- fear of illness
- fear of punishment
- fear of authority
- fear of failure
- fear of the future

Fear shaped:
- religion
- institutions
- family structure
- relationships
- education
- work
- politics

Fear was the invisible architecture of civilization.

But AI, UBI, UBS, and AI dividends collectively dismantle every foundation of fear.

1. Fear of hunger disappears.

UBI + AI dividends guarantee income.

2. Fear of homelessness disappears.

UBS guarantees housing and utilities.

3. Fear of unemployment disappears.

AI becomes the society's labor force.

4. Fear of healthcare costs disappears.

Universal access is guaranteed by public AI.

5. Fear of old age disappears.

Eldercare becomes a democratic right.

6. Fear of inequality disappears.

Wealth concentration collapses under WTT.

7. Fear of ignorance disappears.

AI tutors and universal education lift all people.

8. Fear of irrelevance disappears.

Human purpose is no longer tied to labor.

For the first time, a civilization is built not on fear —
but on freedom from fear.

The Utopia Humanity Society is not utopian in fantasy;
it is utopian in structure.

A civilization without fear

can become a civilization of wisdom.

11.17 The New Human Identity in an AI-Empowered Society

When intelligence becomes universal
and survival becomes guaranteed,
humans must redefine identity itself.

For 300 years, identity = occupation.

"I am a banker."
"I am a teacher."
"I am a builder."
"I am a manager."

But in the post-labor world:

Occupation no longer defines existence.

Humans rediscover who they are
when they are no longer defined by:
- productivity
- market value
- wage labor
- survival pressure

This is the dawn of a new identity framework:

Identity 1 — The Creative Self

When survival is guaranteed,
people create:
- art
- music
- literature
- philosophy
- design
- beauty

Creativity becomes a universal human expression,
not a privilege of the few.

Identity 2 — The Curious Self

AI tutors allow anyone to study:
- mathematics

- history
- physics
- languages
- metaphysics
- economics
- engineering

Lifelong learning becomes natural.
The mind evolves freely.

Identity 3 — The Connected Self

People reconnect with:
- community
- family
- friendship
- collective purpose

When work no longer consumes life,
humans rediscover each other.

Identity 4 — The Conscious Self

Without economic anxiety,
people look inward:
- meditation
- reflection
- spiritual growth
- emotional healing
- self-understanding

A civilization with universal dignity
becomes a civilization of consciousness.

Identity 5 — The Purpose-Driven Self

Humans no longer ask:

"What job must I take to survive?"

They ask:

"What contribution can I make to humanity?"

Purpose replaces pressure.
Meaning replaces fear.
Choice replaces coercion.

Identity 6 — The Planetary Self

Artificial intelligence expands human perspective:
- climate understanding
- ecological awareness
- intergenerational thinking
- global empathy

Humans no longer see themselves as:
- economic units
- national competitors
- labor commodities

They see themselves as:

Guardians of life

and participants in a shared planetary future.

This identity evolution is the true revolution of the 21st century.

11.18 Final Synthesis — Intelligence for All, Forever

Chapter 11 concludes with the ultimate civilizational principle:

Intelligence must be shared

because life is shared.

AI is:
- trained on humanity
- shaped by humanity
- dependent on humanity
- meaningful only within humanity

Thus its benefits must return to humanity.

Public ownership of AI does not stifle innovation.
It multiplies it.

AI dividends do not discourage productivity.
They democratize the gains of productivity.

Public AI utilities do not threaten democracy.
They protect it.

The Wealth Transition Tax does not punish the wealthy.
It stabilizes civilization.

AI becomes:
- the universal teacher
- the universal doctor
- the universal advisor
- the universal assistant
- the universal optimizer
- the universal creative collaborator

But only if its power is democratized.

Only if:
- intelligence is public
- wealth is shared
- dignity is universal
- democracy is preserved
- fear is abolished

Then AI becomes not our master
but our ally.

Not a threat
but a foundation.

Not a replacement for humanity
but an expansion of it.

CHAPTER 12 — REDESIGNING EDUCATION, HEALTHCARE, HOUSING & TRANSPORTATION

How AI Transforms Every System into a Universal Public Right

12.1 Introduction: The End of Industrial-Era Social Systems

The world we live in today is still structured around the logic of the Industrial Revolution:
- schools that mimic factory discipline
- healthcare driven by profit and scarcity
- housing shaped by speculation
- transportation built for fossil-fuel economics

But AI rewrites everything.

In an AI-driven, post-labor civilization:
- information is abundant
- healthcare expertise is infinite
- energy becomes near-zero cost
- construction becomes automated
- planning becomes optimized
- logistics become predictive
- mobility becomes autonomous

The old systems—built on human fear, scarcity, and inequality—collapse under the weight of AI-enabled abundance.

Humanity must not patch these systems.
It must redesign them from the foundation up.

This chapter explains what these redesigned systems look like.

12.2 EDUCATION — From Industrial Schooling to Personalized Lifelong Learning

Industrial-era education was built to produce:
- obedient workers
- uniform knowledge
- predictable labor

- standardized output

Schools prioritized:
- memorization
- compliance
- discipline
- timetable obedience
- silence
- conformity

AI destroys the assumptions behind this system.

AI Makes Industrial Schooling Obsolete

When an AI tutor can:
- teach every subject
- at every level
- in every language
- personalized to every child
- 24 hours a day
- for near-zero cost

The logic of mass classrooms collapses.

12.2.1 Universal AI Tutors

Every child receives a personal AI teacher, capable of:
- assessing strengths and weaknesses
- designing custom learning pathways
- teaching through games, art, music, story
- adjusting pace dynamically
- offering infinite patience
- providing emotional coaching
- eliminating the stigma of "falling behind"

Education becomes:
- personalized
- adaptive
- human-centered
- creative
- joyful

12.2.2 Human Teachers Evolve Into Mentors

Teachers no longer spend:
- 50% of time on discipline
- 30% on administrative work
- 20% on test preparation

Instead, they focus on:
- emotional development
- creativity
- ethics
- leadership skills
- social learning
- conflict resolution
- hands-on discovery

AI handles information delivery.
Humans guide meaning, purpose, and empathy.

12.2.3 Education Becomes a Public Right From Birth to Death

Learning is no longer limited to:
- childhood
- formal schools
- degrees

Instead:

Education is a permanent, lifelong companion.

Adults can seamlessly learn:
- new industries
- new arts
- new philosophies
- science
- engineering
- personal growth

There is no cost barrier.
No time barrier.
No age barrier.

Education becomes infinite and universal.

12.3 HEALTHCARE — From Reactive Treatment to AI-Based Preventive Health

Today's healthcare systems—especially in the U.S.—are built around:
- scarcity
- delay
- financial barriers
- reactive care
- hospital dependence
- insurance bureaucracy
- profit extraction

Healthcare is often least available when most needed.

AI transforms the system into one of abundance.

12.3.1 AI Primary Doctor For Every Citizen

Each person has an AI doctor that:
- monitors health continuously
- performs daily diagnostic scans
- predicts disease before symptoms
- analyzes genetics and lifestyle
- offers personalized nutritional guidance
- flags abnormalities instantly
- contacts human doctors only when needed

Most diseases become:
- predictable
- preventable
- manageable at home

12.3.2 Continuous Monitoring + Zero-Cost Diagnostics

Wearables and sensors allow:
- heart monitoring
- blood oxygen levels
- sleep analysis
- stress detection
- early cancer detection

- infection prediction

Healthcare becomes predictive instead of reactive.

12.3.3 Hospitals Become Centers for Complex Care Only

Routine care disappears.
Hospitals focus on:
- surgery
- advanced procedures
- rare conditions
- trauma care

With AI-assisted robotics, hospitals become:
- faster
- safer
- more accurate

Medical errors—currently the #3 killer in many countries—plummet.

12.3.4 Healthcare Becomes Universal and Zero-Cost

Funding comes from:
- AI dividends
- public AI utilities
- automation taxes
- ultra-wealth taxation
- national AI wealth funds

Healthcare is no longer a commodity.
It is a human right empowered by intelligence.

12.4 HOUSING — From Speculation to Guaranteed Human Shelter

Housing today is defined by:
- speculation
- land monopolies
- mortgages
- exploitation of renters
- homelessness
- poverty traps

AI transforms the housing system entirely.

12.4.1 AI-Assisted Urban Planning

AI can design cities with:
- optimal sunlight
- efficient traffic flow
- maximum green space
- affordable housing density
- minimal noise
- energy efficiency
- community integration

Cities stop being chaotic accidents
and become engineered for human flourishing.

12.4.2 Automated Construction + Zero Waste

Robotics can:
- print houses
- assemble modular units
- perform inspections
- optimize materials
- minimize cost

Housing becomes cheap, fast, and high-quality.

12.4.3 Universal Housing Guarantee

Every citizen receives:
- a home
- utilities
- maintenance
- smart systems
- safety monitoring

Housing is no longer a privilege.
It becomes a baseline civilizational guarantee.

12.4.4 End of Speculation

AI-managed property taxes and public housing supply eliminate:

- rent extraction
- speculative buying
- housing bubbles

Homes stop being investment vehicles
and become human spaces.

12.5 TRANSPORTATION — From Fossil Fuel Chaos to Autonomous Public Mobility

Transportation today is:
- inefficient
- stressful
- dangerous
- environmentally damaging
- centered around private cars
- dominated by fossil fuel interests

AI reverses all of this.

12.5.1 Autonomous Mobility Networks

AI-enabled fleets of:
- autonomous shuttles
- self-driving taxis
- on-demand microbuses
- automated freight systems

eliminate:
- traffic accidents
- drunk driving
- congestion
- driving stress

Transportation becomes:
- smooth
- predictable
- universal
- energy-efficient

12.5.2 AI-Optimized Logistics

Freight becomes:
- perfectly scheduled
- fully automated
- zero waste
- near-zero cost

Costs of goods drop drastically.

12.5.3 Public Transportation Becomes Free

Funding comes from:
- public AI utilities
- national wealth funds
- automation taxes

Mobility becomes a public right, not a luxury.

12.5.4 Ending the Personal Car Era

Private cars become:
- unnecessary
- expensive
- inefficient

Cities gain back:
- 30% more land
- cleaner air
- safer streets
- more parks
- more community spaces

Transportation becomes collective intelligence, not individual burden.

12.6 FOOD SYSTEMS & AGRICULTURE — AI Sustains the Planet

Food has always been shaped by:
- unpredictable weather
- limited land
- labor intensity
- global logistics
- supply chain fragility

AI dissolves nearly all these constraints.

12.6.1 AI-Optimized Agriculture

AI can:
- predict climate patterns
- optimize irrigation
- minimize fertilizer use
- maximize soil health
- prevent crop disease
- direct autonomous tractors
- schedule planting and harvesting

Agriculture becomes:
- sustainable
- resilient
- localized
- resource-efficient

This eliminates the traditional trade-off between:

feeding everyone ⟷ protecting the planet.

12.6.2 Vertical Farming & Urban Food Sovereignty

AI-controlled vertical farms:
- grow food 24/7
- use 95% less water
- require almost no pesticides
- take no farmland
- produce 300%+ yield over traditional farming

Cities become self-sufficient in:
- vegetables
- greens
- fruits
- herbs

Reducing transportation emissions and improving food security.

12.6.3 Autonomous Supply Chains

AI coordinates every step:
- harvesting
- packaging
- transport
- distribution
- retail pricing

This eliminates:
- food waste
- shortages
- supply disruptions

Food becomes abundant and stable.

12.6.4 Universal Access to Nutrition

Every citizen receives:
- guaranteed access to healthy food
- AI-generated personalized nutrition plans
- food assistance based on health profiles
- dietary adjustment for chronic conditions

The concept of hunger becomes obsolete.

12.7 ENERGY — The Move Toward Zero-Cost, Clean Power

Energy today is shaped by:
- fossil fuel dependency

- geopolitical instability
- monopolies
- price volatility
- environmental destruction

AI changes the energy landscape entirely.

12.7.1 AI-Optimized Renewables

AI can dramatically increase:
- solar efficiency
- wind capacity
- hydro stability
- geothermal planning

AI predicts:
- consumption patterns
- maintenance schedules
- peak loads
- weather fluctuations

This creates ultra-stable grids powered by clean energy.

12.7.2 Autonomous Energy Storage

AI directs:
- grid-scale batteries
- local microgrids
- real-time charge-discharge cycles
- distributed storage among neighborhoods

Energy becomes:
- more reliable
- more distributed
- more disaster-resistant

12.7.3 Zero-Cost Marginal Energy

Once renewable infrastructure is built:
- sunlight is free
- wind is free
- geothermal is nearly free

AI ensures:
- maximal efficiency
- minimal downtime
- automated maintenance
- smart transmission

This drives the marginal cost of energy toward zero.

12.7.4 Universal Energy Access

In the Utopia Humanity Society, energy becomes:
- a public right
- universally accessible
- near-zero cost
- sustainably managed

Energy poverty disappears forever.

12.8 PUBLIC SAFETY — AI as Guardian, Not Enforcer

Traditional policing is reactive:
- crime happens
- police respond
- justice arrives late
- communities suffer trauma

AI enables a system of preventive safety without authoritarian intrusion.

12.8.1 Violence Prevention AI

AI monitors:
- conflict patterns

- social stress indicators
- environmental risks
- domestic violence signals
- community tension levels

Intervention is:
- early
- nonviolent
- community-based
- restorative

AI does not become a surveillance tool.
Strict governance prevents misuse.

12.8.2 Justice Becomes Data-Guided, Not Punitive

AI analyzes:
- socio-economic factors
- mental health indicators
- repeat offense predictors
- victim needs

Sentencing evolves from:

"Punish wrongdoers" →
"Prevent future harm."

Justice becomes:
- restorative
- rehabilitative
- evidence-based
- fair

Biases—racial, gender, or economic—are eliminated through transparent auditing.

12.8.3 Community Safety Pods

Local, small, AI-guided safety teams replace militarized police.
They focus on:

- mediation
- mental health intervention
- substance support
- nonviolent crisis response

Violence decreases naturally when:
- inequality falls
- mental health services expand
- community centers thrive
- social support is universal

AI does not enforce power.
AI protects dignity.

12.9 GOVERNANCE — AI-Assisted Democracy, Not Technocracy

AI must never replace democracy.
But AI can upgrade it.

Today's democracies struggle with:
- misinformation
- polarization
- low civic literacy
- manipulation
- slow bureaucracy
- outdated systems

AI helps solve these without undermining citizen authority.

12.9.1 AI-Assisted Legislation

AI analyzes:
- the economic impact of policies
- social effects
- environmental costs
- long-term outcomes
- international comparisons

Lawmakers receive:
- transparent simulations

- statistical projections
- ethical evaluations
- unintended consequence analysis

Policy becomes evidence-based, not ideology-driven.

12.9.2 Digital Citizen Assemblies

AI enables:
- large-scale participation
- structured debates
- multilingual civic engagement
- consensus-building tools

Millions can participate meaningfully.
Democracy becomes participatory at scale.

12.9.3 Transparent Government AI Systems

All AI used by government must be:
- open-source
- auditable
- accountable
- user-visible

No "black box governance."

12.9.4 Bureaucracy Disappears

AI eliminates:
- paperwork
- administrative delays
- redundant processes
- outdated workflows

Public services become:
- instant
- accessible
- transparent

- efficient

Citizens interact with an AI civic interface:
- renew documents
- submit forms
- apply for services
- track rights and benefits

with zero friction.

The state becomes human-centered.

12.10 Final Synthesis — A Civilization Designed for Human Flourishing

With AI enabling abundance across every system:
- education
- healthcare
- housing
- energy
- transportation
- food
- safety
- governance

civilization transforms into something humanity has never experienced before:

A society without fear.

A society without scarcity.

A society without exclusion.

A society where dignity is universal.

A society where intelligence is shared.

A society built for human flourishing.

This is the foundation of the Utopia Humanity Society:
- abundance instead of scarcity
- collectivism without coercion
- equality without authoritarianism

- freedom without insecurity
- prosperity without exploitation
- democracy without ignorance

AI makes the impossible possible.

But only if humanity chooses:

public ownership over private domination
transparency over secrecy
fairness over monopoly
dignity over exploitation
wisdom over fear

When intelligence becomes universal,
so does freedom.

When abundance becomes real,
so does equality.

We are not building a fantasy.
We are building the next civilization.

CHAPTER 13 — LIFE AFTER LABOR: IDENTITY, PURPOSE, AND MEANING

The Human Awakening After the End of Work

13.1 Introduction — The End of the Old Human Story

For 10,000 years, the story of human life was simple:

Work → Survival
Work → Identity
Work → Status
Work → Meaning

People were defined by:
- what they produced
- what job they held
- how much they earned
- how hard they struggled

Entire cultures were built on:
- "hard work is virtue"
- "productivity equals value"
- "rest is laziness"
- "your career is who you are"

But AI ends the economic necessity of human labor.

For the first time in history:

Work is no longer required for survival.

Not because humans became weaker —
but because machines became strong enough
to carry the burden of production.

Humanity stands at the threshold of a profound shift:

We must rediscover what it means to be human

when we are no longer workers.

This is not a technological question.
This is a spiritual question.
A civilizational question.
A question of identity.

The 21st century demands a new answer.

13.2 The Death of "Labor = Identity"

Before AI, identity was tied almost entirely to occupation:

"I am a lawyer."
"I am a construction worker."
"I am a nurse."
"I am a manager."
"I am a programmer."

Work became:
- social hierarchy
- self-worth
- dignity
- meaning
- belonging

But this model has always been flawed:
- It reduces humans to economic units.
- It defines life by output.
- It ignores creativity.
- It suppresses individuality.
- It punishes those who cannot work.

AI exposes the truth:

Humans are more than their labor.

When machines can:
- build
- analyze
- diagnose
- strategize
- write
- design
- compute
- manage

then human value must come from somewhere deeper —
from qualities machines cannot replace:
- empathy
- imagination
- intuition
- presence
- emotional depth
- spirituality
- relational intelligence
- moral judgment
- artistic expression

The end of labor is not a loss.
It is a return.

A return to the human essence
that industrial society ignored.

13.3 The Psychological Crisis of Post-Labor Transition

The end of labor creates a paradox:

Material abundance increases,

but psychological stability decreases — at first.

Because for many, work provided:
- structure
- routine
- identity
- community
- validation
- purpose

When these disappear, people may experience:
- existential anxiety
- loss of direction
- fear of purposelessness
- identity confusion
- social isolation
- meaninglessness

This is not a failure of the individual.
This is the residue of an outdated civilization.

People were conditioned to believe:

"Your worth comes from what you produce."

When that belief collapses, humans must rebuild meaning
on a foundation not dependent on productivity.

The Utopia Humanity Society prepares for this psychological transition
by offering:
- mentorship
- creativity training
- community networks
- AI-guided self-discovery
- lifelong education pathways
- emotional development programs
- purpose-building workshops
- philosophy and meaning curricula
- spiritual and reflective practices
- universal social belonging programs

The end of labor is not the end of purpose.
It is the beginning of true purpose.

13.4 The Five New Foundations of Identity in a Post-Labor World

Once survival is guaranteed,
identity emerges from five new sources:

Foundation 1: Self-Discovery

People ask:
- Who am I without economic pressure?
- What do I genuinely enjoy?
- What makes me feel alive?
- What am I curious about?
- What do I want to create?

AI assists this through:
- personality mapping
- interest exploration
- emotional resonance analysis
- guided introspection
- creative recommendations

For most people, this is the first time
they truly meet themselves.

Foundation 2: Creativity and Expression

Creativity becomes the primary mode of human expression:
- art
- writing
- dance
- filmmaking
- design

- music
- theater
- world-building
- virtual environments

AI does not replace creativity.
It amplifies it.

Every individual becomes:
- creator
- storyteller
- artist
- inventor

The arts expand into a new Renaissance.

Foundation 3: Contribution and Service

Humans naturally seek:
- to help
- to uplift
- to inspire
- to protect
- to lead
- to guide
- to teach

Without economic pressure,
people contribute because:
- they care
- they feel called
- they want meaning
- they want connection

Work becomes a gift,
not a requirement.

Foundation 4: Relationships and Community

In a post-labor world, people prioritize:
- family
- friendships
- love
- community gatherings
- shared meals
- collective projects
- festivals
- local culture

Social bonds strengthen
because time is abundant
and fear is gone.

When people are no longer exhausted or financially stressed,
they can finally show up for each other.

Foundation 5: Growth and Inner Development

Humans turn inward to explore:
- spirituality
- philosophy
- meditation
- emotional literacy
- healing
- moral development
- ethical reflection
- self-awareness

Machines handle the external world.
Humans cultivate the internal world.

The species matures psychologically and spiritually.

13.5 The Three Modes of Post-Labor Purpose

In the Utopia Humanity Society,
purpose emerges in three intertwined modes:

Mode A: Creative Purpose

The purpose of:
- making
- designing
- imagining
- storytelling
- innovating
- expressing

AI becomes a canvas for infinite creativity.

Greater creativity → deeper meaning → deeper identity.

Mode B: Relational Purpose

The purpose of:
- love
- friendship
- mentorship
- caregiving
- community
- partnership
- collective joy

Relationships become the true measure of a meaningful life.

Mode C: Existential Purpose

The purpose of:
- understanding the universe
- exploring consciousness
- pursuing wisdom
- expanding human awareness
- living authentically
- discovering one's unique path

For the first time in history,
every human has access to:
- philosophy
- psychology
- art
- science
- spiritual traditions
- reflective practices

Purpose becomes a universal right.

13.6 The Human Flourishing Curve

During the transition to post-labor society,
humans experience three phases:

Phase 1 — Decompression

(Years 1–3 after liberation from economic labor)

People rest.
People recover.
People sleep.
People breathe.

Centuries of exhaustion unravel.

There is no productivity pressure.
No guilt for resting.

This phase is necessary for healing.

Phase 2 — Exploration

(Years 3–7)

People explore:
- interests
- passions
- relationships
- creative fields
- knowledge domains
- physical environments

AI assists self-discovery through:
- guided exploration
- emotional resonance mapping
- interest simulations
- virtual apprenticeships

This phase is curiosity reborn.

Phase 3 — Flourishing

(Year 7 onward)

People find:
- meaning
- purpose
- community
- contribution
- creativity
- inner peace

This is not utopia as fantasy.
This is utopia as psychology:

The human mind flourishes
when freed from economic coercion.

13.7 The Role of AI in Human Purpose: Enhancer, Not Replacer

AI becomes:
- collaborator
- advisor
- muse
- assistant
- amplifier
- coach
- companion

AI cannot:
- feel emotion
- seek meaning
- create moral value
- experience beauty
- form spiritual awareness

Humans remain the source of:
- purpose
- values
- ethics
- culture
- consciousness

AI expands capacity,
but humans define direction.

AI clears the obstacles.
Humans walk the path.

13.8 The Evolution of Relationships in a Post-Labor Civilization

When labor disappears as the organizing force of society, relationships take the central role.

In industrial civilization, relationships were often constrained by:
- exhaustion
- long commutes
- financial dependency
- insecurity
- time scarcity
- workplace stress
- fear of the future

In the Utopia Humanity Society, these constraints dissolve.

People can finally form relationships from:
- authenticity
- emotional alignment
- shared values
- mutual support
- genuine choice

instead of:
- financial necessity
- social pressure
- survival incentives

13.8.1 Love Without Economic Pressure

Traditional relationships often contained:
- breadwinner hierarchy
- financial control
- gendered dependence
- economic bargaining
- transactional roles

In a post-labor society:
- everyone has UBI
- everyone has housing
- healthcare is universal
- AI dividends guarantee stability

Therefore:

Love becomes voluntary, not transactional.

Relationships become partnerships of equals.

People choose each other for:
- emotional resonance
- shared dreams
- companionship
- spiritual growth
- joy

not because they need:
- income
- stability
- support
- childcare labor
- survival

This creates the most authentic relationships in human history.

13.8.2 Friendship as a Core Life Structure

Friendships deepen because:
- time is abundant
- community is valued
- loneliness is reduced
- shared activities flourish

People spend more time:

- hosting gatherings
- joining creative circles
- participating in community rituals
- collaborating on projects
- traveling together
- learning together

Friendship becomes not secondary but central.

13.8.3 Community as a Source of Identity

Communities shift from geographic
to purpose-driven:
- artistic communities
- ecological communities
- spiritual collectives
- science and discovery groups
- wellness-oriented communities
- cultural preservation circles
- global online affinity groups

Humans no longer define themselves by their employer.
They define themselves by:
- who they connect with
- what they create
- what they explore
- what brings meaning

Community replaces corporation
as the center of life.

13.9 The Rise of Play, Joy, and Human Aliveness

Throughout history, play was considered:
- childish
- unproductive

- inappropriate for adults
- a distraction from work

But play is:
- creativity
- experimentation
- presence
- joy
- embodiment
- connection

AI-driven abundance reclaims play as a pillar of civilization.

13.9.1 Play Becomes a Cultural Value

Adults engage in:
- music
- dance
- sport
- exploration
- performance
- gaming
- collaborative storytelling
- virtual experiences
- physical adventures

Not as escape,
but as expression.

13.9.2 Joy as a Metric of Social Success

Governments stop measuring:
- GDP
- output
- hours worked

They begin measuring:

- joy
- wellbeing
- meaning
- community health
- psychological flourishing

A society that is safe, stable, and abundant
has no reason to suppress joy.

Joy becomes a form of wisdom.

13.9.3 AI as the Catalyst of Play

AI enables:
- immersive realities
- new artistic mediums
- personalized experiences
- real-time creative collaboration

AI becomes:
- a playmate
- a tool for imagination
- a companion for exploration

Human aliveness expands.

13.10 The Return of Philosophy and Spirituality

When survival no longer consumes life,
humans naturally turn toward deeper questions:
- What is consciousness?
- What is a good life?
- How should we treat one another?
- What is the purpose of existence?
- What is beauty?
- What is truth?

For centuries, these questions were confined to:
- monasteries
- universities
- intellectual elites

But in the post-labor civilization,
philosophy becomes universal.

13.10.1 Philosophy as Daily Practice

People receive:
- AI-guided philosophy dialogues
- moral reasoning exercises
- reflective journaling prompts
- meditative frameworks

People learn to think:
- deeply
- ethically
- spiritually
- compassionately

The ability to choose one's own worldview
becomes a universal right.

13.10.2 Spirituality Without Dogma

AI empowers individuals to explore:
- Buddhism
- Stoicism
- Taoism
- Sufism
- Christianity
- Secular humanism
- Mindfulness traditions
- Indigenous wisdom
- Modern consciousness studies

without rigid institutions
or authoritarian structures.

Spirituality becomes:
- experiential
- personal
- reflective
- evolutionary

Humans rediscover awe —
the emotion that industrial capitalism suppressed.

13.10.3 The Rise of Contemplative Intelligence

With emotional AI and reflective assistants,
humans learn to:
- observe their minds
- heal trauma
- develop compassion
- practice gratitude
- cultivate awareness

The civilization becomes not only wealthier
but wiser.

13.11 The End of Loneliness

Loneliness today is a global epidemic.
Ironically, it is most common in:
- rich countries
- large cities
- hyper-individualistic societies

AI-driven abundance offers structural solutions.

13.11.1 Loneliness Ends When Time Is Abundant

When people are no longer:
- overworked
- exhausted
- financially stressed

they have time to nurture relationships.

13.11.2 AI Helps People Connect

AI recommends:
- compatible friendships
- local groups
- shared activities
- emotional communication tools

AI facilitates community formation —
not as a substitute for human connection,
but as a bridge to it.

13.11.3 Community Infrastructure Eliminates Isolation

Public spaces become:
- open
- abundant
- beautiful
- inclusive

Cities shift from car-centered
to community-centered.

Every citizen has access to:
- community gardens
- shared kitchens
- learning centers

- parks
- creative labs
- meditation halls
- studios
- maker spaces

Humans rediscover the joy of belonging.

13.12 The New Human Narrative

Every civilization has a story.

For 10,000 years, the story was:

"You must work to survive."

In the AI-driven Utopia Humanity Society, the new story becomes:

"You exist to flourish."

The Old Narrative:
- Work defines you.
- Money determines worth.
- Scarcity is normal.
- Fear is necessary.
- Competition drives progress.
- Success is rare.
- Rest is shameful.

The New Narrative:
- You are more than labor.
- Your worth is inherent.
- Abundance is achievable.
- Fear is obsolete.
- Cooperation drives progress.
- Flourishing is universal.

- Rest is sacred.

Human identity evolves from:

worker → citizen → creator → explorer → conscious being

13.13 Final Synthesis — A Civilization That Redefines Life Itself

Life after labor is not the end of purpose.
It is the liberation of purpose.

Humans become:
- freer
- wiser
- more creative
- more connected
- more joyful
- more compassionate
- more reflective
- more alive

AI does not diminish humanity.
It expands it.

When machines take over labor,
humans finally become human.

The Utopia Humanity Society is built on one principle:

Humans do not exist to serve the economy.

The economy exists to serve human flourishing.

This chapter closes with the central truth:

The end of labor is not the end of meaning.

It is the beginning of a new civilization
where every human life becomes a work of art.

CHAPTER 14 — DEMOCRACY IN THE AGE OF AI

Preserving Freedom in a World of Infinite Intelligence

14.1 Introduction — The Greatest Political Challenge in Human History

Democracy was created in a world where:
- information traveled slowly
- decisions were made locally
- citizens could understand the issues
- institutions were stable
- elites had limited reach
- manipulation was constrained by geography

But AI introduces:
- instant communication
- algorithmic persuasion
- infinite-scale manipulation
- hyper-targeted propaganda
- deepfake political chaos
- cognitive influence at population scale
- automated narrative warfare
- instant misinformation distribution
- emotional modeling of society

This is not an incremental change.

This is a civilizational rupture.

AI can break democracy
by overwhelming the cognitive capacity of citizens.

But AI can also save democracy
by empowering citizens with intelligence, transparency, and accountability.

The difference is not technological.

The difference is political design.
This chapter explains how the Utopia Humanity Society ensures that AI strengthens democracy instead of destroying it.

14.2 Why Traditional Democracy Fails in the AI Century

Modern democracies are already struggling with:
- polarization
- misinformation
- voter disengagement
- corporate influence
- media fragmentation
- declining trust
- economic inequality
- bureaucratic rigidity
- manipulation by elites
- foreign interference

AI amplifies these weak points.

14.2.1 Misinformation at Machine Scale

AI can produce:
- fake news
- synthetic videos
- forged speeches
- fabricated scandals
- impersonated voices
- artificially generated protests
- algorithmically tailored propaganda

Humans cannot detect these on their own.

14.2.2 Cognitive Overload

The human brain evolved to:
- track small tribes

- process slow information
- manage local affairs

AI overwhelms cognition:
- too many data streams
- too many narratives
- too many choices
- too much complexity

Citizens become overwhelmed,
leading to apathy or blind trust.

14.2.3 Elite Capture

Without regulation, AI becomes controlled by:
- corporations
- billionaires
- political machines
- intelligence agencies

They can manipulate public opinion invisibly.

Democracy collapses from the inside.

14.3 The UHS Response — AI-Assisted Democracy

The Utopia Humanity Society does not reject AI.
It integrates AI into democracy with constitutional safeguards.

Democracy becomes:
- more informed
- more participatory
- more transparent
- more intelligent
- more secure

AI becomes a public tool — not a private weapon.

Below are the core innovations.

14.4 The Citizen Intelligence Layer

Every citizen receives access to a democratic AI companion:
- unbiased
- factual
- contextual
- transparent
- safe
- constitutionally protected

This AI companion:
- explains policies in simple language
- identifies misinformation
- provides evidence-based summaries
- compares proposals across history
- shows international examples
- reveals economic consequences
- checks political claims
- highlights manipulation techniques
- suggests critical thinking questions

Citizens become super-informed, not manipulated.

This alone increases democratic capacity by 10×.

14.5 AI-Guided Civic Literacy for All

Civic knowledge becomes universal through:
- personalized learning modules
- interactive simulations
- scenario-based political education
- historical case studies
- AI-driven Socratic dialogue

People learn how to think democratically:
- How do institutions work?
- What is constitutional law?
- What is a budget?
- What is propaganda?
- How do elections function?
- What are citizens' rights?
- How do we evaluate evidence?

A democracy with an educated electorate becomes nearly indestructible.

14.6 The Transparent AI Governance Core

Government AI systems must be:
- open-source
- explainable
- auditable
- accountable
- monitored by citizens

No closed AI can influence political decision-making.

All political AI actions must be:
- logged
- reversible
- reviewable
- subject to oversight

The public must always know:
- How was a decision reached?
- What data was used?
- What alternatives were considered?
- Which biases were tested?
- Who authorized the process?

Transparency becomes absolute.

14.7 AI-Assisted Lawmaking — Evidence Instead of Ideology

AI models simulate:
- economic impact
- environmental consequences
- social outcomes
- risk scenarios
- long-term projections
- international comparisons

Before passing any law, lawmakers receive:
- an AI-generated evidence brief
- side-by-side policy alternatives
- cost-benefit analysis
- harm forecasts
- ethical implications

This eliminates:
- ignorance
- misinformation
- blind ideology

Legislation becomes rational, not partisan.

14.8 Digital Citizen Assemblies

AI enables large-scale democracy:

Millions can participate in:
- debates
- deliberation
- proposal creation
- priority voting
- policy refinement

AI organizes debates by:
- clustering viewpoints

- identifying consensus
- translating languages
- highlighting key disagreements

Citizens see:
- where the majority actually stands
- where minority concerns lie
- how compromise can form

This makes democracy collective, not passive.

14.9 Preventing AI Monopolies from Controlling Democracy

The Utopia Humanity Society enacts
the strongest anti-monopoly protections in human history:

A. No private ownership of foundational models

All foundation AI is public.

B. No corporate-funded political AI

All political persuasion AI is illegal.

C. Mandatory public audits of all political algorithms

D. 90% tax on AI monopoly profits

E. Break up or nationalize any entity that endangers democratic integrity

AI power must always remain in the hands of society.

14.10 Preventing Authoritarian Capture

Democracy can be destroyed by:
- strongmen
- populists
- militaries
- corporations
- political parties

The UHS prevents this through:

1. AI Oversight Council with No Political Members

Cannot be influenced by elections or parties.

2. Citizen Right to Audit Government AI

Every model — fully transparent.

3. Multi-node governance

No single institution can control AI.

4. Constitutional ban on surveillance AI

No Chinese-style digital authoritarianism.

5. AI-verified elections

Transparent, auditable, fraud-proof.

6. Decentralized digital identity

No central government database can control lives.

7. Public emergency override

Citizens can vote to suspend unsafe AI systems.

Democracy becomes resilient, not fragile.

14.11 Elections in the AI Century

Elections become:
- clean
- transparent
- accessible
- misinformation-free

AI Enhances Elections by:
1. Flagging misinformation in real time
2. Verifying candidates' claims
3. Providing neutral summaries of positions
4. Offering fact-based comparisons
5. Translating all political content
6. Providing accessible debate analysis
7. Conducting secure electronic voting
8. Ensuring vote-count integrity

Citizens become empowered voters, not manipulated targets.

14.12 The Return of Trust in Public Life

Trust collapses in societies where:
- inequality grows
- corruption spreads
- misinformation dominates
- corporate power expands

But trust returns in societies where:
- public wealth is shared
- AI is transparent
- data is protected
- democracy is participatory
- inequality is addressed

- public goods are universal

The Utopia Humanity Society rebuilds trust
by redesigning the information environment itself.

AI becomes a tool for clarity, not deception.

Democracy becomes a process of collective intelligence, not collective confusion.

14.13 Final Synthesis — Democracy Reborn Through Intelligence

AI is not the enemy of democracy.
Ignorance is.

AI is not a threat to freedom.
Concentrated power is.

AI is not a danger to society.
Unregulated capitalism and authoritarianism are.

When AI is:
- publicly owned
- transparently governed
- universally accessible
- ethically constrained
- democratically monitored

it becomes the greatest democratic innovation since the invention of literacy.

The Utopia Humanity Society transforms democracy from:

a fragile system into a resilient, intelligent, participatory, informed civilization.

The chapter concludes with the central truth:

AI will not replace democracy.

AI will complete it.

CHAPTER 15 — PLANETARY STEWARDSHIP & THE REGENERATIVE CIVILIZATION

How AI Enables Humanity to Heal the Earth and Build a Self-Sustaining Future

15.1 Introduction — The End of the Extractive Era

For 300 years, human progress was built on extraction:
- extracting labor
- extracting resources
- extracting energy
- extracting land
- extracting time
- extracting health
- extracting community
- extracting future generations' well-being

Capitalism, designed in an era of scarcity, treated the planet as:
- an infinite warehouse
- a bottomless trash bin
- a silent servant
- a resource to be consumed for profit

Industrial civilization succeeded economically
but failed ecologically.

Humanity pushed Earth to crisis:
- climate change
- mass extinction
- soil degradation
- ocean collapse
- pollution everywhere
- extreme weather
- water scarcity
- ecosystem disruption

The old economic model — based on endless growth and endless consumption — has reached a mathematically unavoidable end.

And then AI arrived.

AI did *not* create these problems.
But AI is the first technology powerful enough to help humanity heal them.

The Utopia Humanity Society marks the historical transition from:

Extraction → Regeneration
Consumption → Stewardship
Short-term profit → Long-term care
Human-centered growth → Planet-centered flourishing

This chapter explains how.

15.2 Why AI Makes Regenerative Civilization Possible

Before AI, planetary stewardship was limited by:
- human cognitive limits
- slow data processing
- unpredictable environments
- economic constraints
- political resistance
- fragmented global systems

AI removes these constraints.

AI Can Monitor the Entire Planet in Real Time

AI can:
- track deforestation
- model climate patterns
- predict ecosystem collapse
- map biodiversity

- analyze ocean currents
- detect pollution
- optimize agriculture
- design conservation zones

Not through guesswork,
but through continuous planetary sensing.

AI Can Optimize Resource Use Globally

AI can reduce:
- water waste
- food waste
- energy waste
- material waste

through:
- predictive modeling
- autonomous logistics
- dynamic pricing
- adaptive supply chains

AI Enables Post-Scarcity Economics

When:
- energy becomes near-zero cost
- food becomes abundant
- manufacturing becomes automated
- work becomes optional
- inequality collapses
- public goods become universal

Then ecological healing becomes politically possible.

Societies no longer fear:
- job loss in fossil fuel sectors
- GDP slowdown
- economic collapse

- political instability

AI abundance removes scarcity psychology —
the root of ecological destruction.

15.3 The Post-Carbon Transformation

The Utopia Humanity Society transitions from fossil fuels to renewable abundance through AI-enabled pathways.

15.3.1 AI-Optimized Renewable Energy

AI manages:
- solar grids
- wind farms
- geothermal networks
- tidal power
- energy storage
- microgrids

Energy becomes:
- clean
- affordable
- reliable
- decentralized
- resilient

15.3.2 Autonomous Infrastructure Transition

AI coordinates:
- shutting down coal plants
- upgrading transmission lines
- deploying new renewable sites
- retraining former workers
- managing energy demand shifts

The transition becomes smooth instead of chaotic.

15.3.3 Decentralized Energy Democracy

Every community becomes:
- energy producer
- energy steward
- energy beneficiary

No more:
- fossil oligarchies
- geopolitical energy wars
- energy poverty

Energy abundance eliminates one of the key causes of conflict.

15.4 The Regeneration Economy — Healing What Was Destroyed

Once AI removes the pressures of scarcity,
society can focus on repairing the planet.

The regeneration economy includes:
- reforesting depleted lands
- restoring coral reefs
- reviving rivers and wetlands
- healing soil
- rebuilding biodiversity corridors
- cleaning oceans
- rewilding ecosystems
- reversing desertification
- restoring pollinator networks

15.4.1 AI Restoration Mapping

AI creates:
- hyper-precise ecological restoration plans
- long-term climate adaptation models
- species distribution forecasts
- optimal rewilding strategies

No previous civilization had this capability.

15.4.2 Autonomous Regeneration Systems

Drones, robotics, and autonomous systems:
- plant billions of trees
- release beneficial species
- monitor soil microbiomes
- clean microplastics
- repair coral structures
- irrigate drylands
- reinforce coastlines

AI supervises the planet like a doctor treating a patient —
not with domination,
but with care.

15.4.3 Human Participation in Healing

Humans join:
- ecological volunteer networks
- regenerative agriculture communities
- conservation projects
- climate-adaptation teams
- river and forest stewardship programs

This becomes a new form of civic pride.
Regeneration is not a chore —
it is a collective spiritual act.

15.5 AI-Guided Urban Rewilding & City Transformation

Human cities have been designed for:
- cars
- profit
- speed
- consumption

- density
- economic output

Not for:
- health
- joy
- ecology
- community
- mental well-being

AI redesigns entire urban ecosystems.

15.5.1 Cities Move From Concrete to Green

Under AI optimization:
- streets become gardens
- rooftops become farms
- buildings become carbon sinks
- public spaces become forests
- urban heat islands disappear

Cities shift from heat engines to ecosystems.

15.5.2 AI-Directed Water Cycles

AI manages:
- flood control
- aquifer recharge
- stormwater routing
- water purification
- drought prevention

Water becomes abundant and clean.

15.5.3 Pollution-Free Mobility

Self-driving public mobility eliminates:
- car pollution

- traffic deaths
- congestion
- noise

Cities become walkable, breathable, joyful.

15.6 AI as Planetary Guardian — Without Becoming a Planetary Tyrant

The greatest challenge:

How do we use AI to protect the Earth

without allowing AI to dominate humanity?

The Utopia Humanity Society uses strict governance:

1. AI monitors ecosystems — not people.

Environmental data is collected, not personal surveillance.

2. AI recommendations are transparent.

All ecological advice is public.

3. Humans make the final decisions.

AI is advisory, not authoritative.

4. Ecosystem rights are encoded in law.

Nature becomes a legal stakeholder.

5. Citizens can override AI environmental decisions

through democratic processes.

AI becomes the guardian of planetary systems,
not the guardian *over* humans.

15.7 Universal Ecological Citizenship

Citizenship expands to include:
- responsibility for ecosystems
- contribution to preservation
- participation in restoration
- education on ecological intelligence
- AI-assisted environmental literacy

Every person becomes:
- steward
- protector
- participant
- contributor

The Earth is no longer a backdrop
but a living partner.

15.8 Post-Scarcity Economics Means Post-Scarcity Ecology

A society without economic scarcity can finally treat the planet with compassion.

No more:

"Jobs vs. environment."
"Growth vs. nature."
"Profit vs. health."
"Economy vs. climate."

In the Utopia Humanity Society:
- growth is decoupled from destruction
- prosperity is decoupled from pollution

- wealth is decoupled from exploitation

AI unlocks the first economic model
where healing the planet increases wealth.

15.9 The Earth as a Partner, Not a Resource

Humanity evolves from:
- domination → cooperation
- extraction → regeneration
- superiority → humility
- consumption → stewardship
- separation → interdependence

The new ethics says:

The Earth is not property.

The Earth is a relationship.

AI helps humanity understand:
- complex ecosystems
- fragile interdependencies
- long-term planetary cycles
- the consequences of human decisions

Humans finally see themselves
not as masters of nature
but as participants in its continuity.

15.10 Global Climate Coordination Using AI

Climate change today is not a technological failure —
it is a coordination failure.
- nations compete instead of collaborate
- policies move slower than climate physics

- data is fragmented
- responsibilities are unclear
- no global enforcement mechanism exists

AI changes this by creating a planetary coordination layer.

15.10.1 The Global Climate Intelligence Network (GCIN)

A publicly governed, decentralized AI system that:
- monitors global emissions
- predicts climate thresholds
- analyzes country-specific risks
- evaluates policy effectiveness
- simulates future scenarios
- identifies optimal interventions
- coordinates disaster response

This network is:
- open
- transparent
- democratic
- non-militarized
- non-corporate

Humanity receives a shared "dashboard"
of the planet's health.

Climate becomes a collective responsibility,
not a geopolitical weapon.

15.10.2 AI-Driven Climate Agreements

Current treaties rely on:
- voluntary pledges
- political promises
- inconsistent reporting

AI creates:
- real-time verification
- automated emissions tracking
- transparent national reporting
- dynamic adjustment mechanisms
- global non-compliance alerts

Countries cannot hide data
or manipulate climate reports.

Trust becomes measurable.

15.10.3 AI-Optimized Climate Solutions

AI identifies:
- best places to reforest
- best ways to reduce urban heat
- best renewable energy mix
- best water reclamation strategies
- best ocean restoration zones

Climate action becomes:
- faster
- smarter
- cheaper
- more scalable

AI makes climate restoration physically possible
and politically unavoidable.

15.11 AI and the Prevention of Resource Wars

Throughout history, nations have fought over:
- oil
- land
- minerals

- water
- trade routes
- energy resources

AI reduces or eliminates every cause of resource conflict.

15.11.1 Renewable Abundance Reduces Energy Wars

When energy is:
- local
- renewable
- abundant
- decentralized

there is no need for:
- oil wars
- pipeline geopolitics
- energy colonization

AI ends the logic of petro-conflict.

15.11.2 Autonomous Food Systems Reduce Agricultural Wars

Food becomes:
- abundant
- hyper-efficient
- climate-resilient
- locally produced

Nations no longer invade for farmland
or monopolize grain routes.

15.11.3 AI-Based Water Management Prevents Water Conflicts

AI predicts:
- drought

- aquifer depletion
- river flow changes
- oceanic salt shifts
- glacier melt

AI coordinates:
- global water-sharing agreements
- sustainable irrigation
- desalination strategies
- ecological restoration

Water wars lose their logic.

15.11.4 Transparent Global Supply Chains Prevent Exploitation

AI reveals:
- illegal mining
- resource hoarding
- corruption networks
- smuggling routes
- environmental abuses

Transparency eliminates hidden extraction.

15.12 The Biodiversity Renaissance

Earth is experiencing its sixth mass extinction.
But the Utopia Humanity Society brings forth
a *Biodiversity Renaissance*.

15.12.1 AI Biodiversity Mapping

AI identifies:
- collapsing species
- genetic vulnerabilities
- migration shifts

- habitat fragmentation
- poaching patterns
- invasive species risks

This informs rapid intervention.

15.12.2 AI-Designed Wildlife Corridors

AI calculates optimal corridor locations
to reconnect:
- forests
- rivers
- wetlands
- mountain ranges

allowing species to move safely
across restored ecosystems.

15.12.3 Autonomous Rewilding Teams

Drones and robotics restore ecosystems:
- planting pollinator meadows
- rebuilding coral structures
- introducing keystone species
- controlling invasive organisms
- regenerating soil microbiomes

This accelerates natural processes
that would otherwise take centuries.

15.12.4 Genetic Preservation and Revitalization

AI supports:
- conservation genomics
- species revival where ethical

* hybrid resilience strategies
* disease prevention in wildlife

The Earth's living network becomes resilient again.

15.13 The Intergenerational Contract

Humanity has historically failed
future generations.

Children inherited:
* polluted air
* degraded land
* rising seas
* collapsing biodiversity
* economic inequality
* political instability

The Utopia Humanity Society establishes
a new Intergenerational Contract.

15.13.1 AI Protects Long-Term Interests

AI models consider:
* 50-year outlook
* 100-year climate impacts
* multigenerational resource use
* long-term infrastructure stability
* demographic transitions

Humans vote on short-term issues.
AI projects long-term consequences.

Policy becomes future-proofed.

15.13.2 Children As Rights Holders

Children gain constitutional rights:
- clean air
- stable climate
- ecological inheritance
- access to AI education
- future economic security
- public wealth benefits

The unborn are considered stakeholders.

15.13.3 The 100-Year Civilization Plan

Every generation contributes to:
- ecological health
- cultural continuity
- technological responsibility
- moral development

Instead of short-term politics,
humanity adopts long-term stewardship.

15.14 The Planetary Constitution

Humanity requires a new foundational document —
a constitution not only for nations,
but for the Earth itself.

15.14.1 Rights of Nature

The Planetary Constitution recognizes:
- rivers as legal persons
- forests as guardianship entities
- ecosystems as stakeholders
- species as protected communities

Nature receives legal standing —
not symbolic,
but enforceable.

15.14.2 Global AI Governance Principles

The constitution restricts AI:
- no militarized autonomous AI
- no surveillance authoritarianism
- no corporate control of intelligence
- mandatory transparency
- public audits
- ethical training data requirements
- human override rights

AI becomes a tool of liberation,
not domination.

15.14.3 Universal Ecological Duties

Citizens have responsibilities:
- protect ecosystems
- reduce harm
- participate in collective restoration
- maintain environmental literacy

Stewardship becomes a civic identity.

15.14.4 Global Solidarity as Constitutional Principle

We shift from:
- "my nation first" to
- "humanity and Earth first."

This ends the logic of nationalism

as a destructive force.

15.15 Final Synthesis — A Civilizational Harmony Between Humanity and Earth

Human civilization has passed through three eras:

1. The Survival Era

(humans vs. nature)

2. The Industrial Era

(humans overpowering nature)

3. The Regenerative Era (Utopia Humanity Society)

(humans co-evolving with nature)

AI abundance allows humanity to:
- heal what was broken
- restore ecological balance
- guarantee universal dignity
- eliminate resource scarcity
- prevent wars
- align with Earth rather than dominate it

The new civilization is defined by one principle:

Human flourishing and planetary flourishing

are the same goal.

We no longer choose between:
- humans or nature
- prosperity or ecology
- growth or sustainability

AI ends the false dichotomy.

Everything becomes integrated:
- ecology
- economy
- community
- technology
- democracy
- human purpose

For the first time,
humanity acts as a planetary species
with the intelligence to care for its home.

The chapter closes with the vision:

A civilization that heals the Earth

is a civilization worthy of surviving.

The Utopia Humanity Society
is not the end of history.
It is the beginning of humanity's
first truly wise era.

EPILOGUE — THE FIRST DAY OF THE NEW CIVILIZATION

A story of waking up in the Utopia Humanity Society

No one remembers the exact moment
when the old world finally ended.

There was no explosion,
no revolution,
no single day of triumph or collapse.

Civilizations rarely fall in a single instant.
They dissolve quietly,
like long-held beliefs losing their grip on the mind.

But almost everyone remembers
the first morning
they woke up
and realized something had changed.

It was not the buildings.
Not the streets.
Not the architecture of cities.

It was the atmosphere itself —
a kind of lightness,
as if the air had finally exhaled
after centuries of holding its breath.

This is the story of one such morning.

1. The Awakening

It begins with a simple experience.

You open your eyes.

There is no alarm clock ringing.
No weight on your chest.
No urgent pressure from the world.
No silent scream from a calendar asking for your labor.

The morning feels…
spacious.

You stretch,
and for a moment you feel disoriented
because your body does not remember
what it is like to wake up
without the invisible hand of survival
pushing you into motion.

The old tension isn't there.

The fear of falling behind
is gone.
The financial anxiety
is silent.
The rush to produce
for someone else
has evaporated.

You breathe.

You feel the unfamiliar sensation
of being alive
without being demanded.

This is the first day
of the new civilization.

2. The World Outside the Window

You walk to the window.

Outside, the city looks familiar
yet entirely transformed:
- no rush-hour traffic
- no horns
- no exhaust
- no crowds of exhausted commuters

Instead:
- autonomous shuttles moving silently
- green walkways
- sunlight bouncing off rooftop farms
- children playing in a community garden
- neighbors talking
- the distant hum of clean energy

The city feels alive —
not as a machine,
but as an organism.

You realize something:
the world is no longer built
around economic fear
but around human flourishing.

For the first time in your life,
you do not feel extracted from.
You feel supported by.

3. The AI Companion

Your AI companion greets you gently:

"Good morning.

Would you like today to be a day of exploration,
creation,
connection,
or rest?"

Not a command.
Not a schedule.
A question.

A question that recognizes you
as a person with agency,
not a unit of production.

You ask:

"What do I need today?"

The AI responds with a warmth
that is not emotional
but deeply respectful:

"Your body is well-rested.
Your mind is calm.
Your curiosity is elevated.
Perhaps today is a day for learning
or creating beauty."

A strange feeling arises in you:
you are not being optimized
for profit or output.
You are being guided
toward flourishing.

4. Walking Through the Community

You step outside.

On the street:
- an elderly man practices tai chi with an AI-assisted posture guide
- teenagers collaborate on a public art project
- a mother and daughter plant herbs in a shared garden
- a disabled woman moves freely with an exoskeleton

designed as a public right, not a luxury

No one is rushing.
No one is desperate.
No one is left behind.

You feel something unfamiliar:

trust.

Trust in the world.
Trust in others.
Trust in yourself.
Trust that you belong
and will always belong.

5. Moments of Meaning

At a community hall, you see:
- a class on poetry
- a workshop on conflict resolution
- an open circle discussing planetary stewardship
- a group painting a mural representing

the "Intergenerational Contract"
- a choir rehearsing a piece composed collaboratively

with AI and humans

These are not hobbies squeezed into the edges of life.
These are the center of life.

Meaning is no longer a private rebellion

against capitalism.
Meaning is a public right.

6. The Absence of Fear

You feel a sudden awareness —
like noticing the absence of a sound
that had been humming in the background
your whole life.

The fear is gone.

Not the primal fear of survival in the wild,
but the manufactured fear of modernity:

- fear of unemployment
- fear of medical bills
- fear of homelessness
- fear of being unproductive
- fear of being useless
- fear of falling behind
- fear of not having value

That fear has been designed out of society
the way polio was designed out of the world:

through
intelligence,
compassion,
and the moral courage to redesign civilization.

You whisper to yourself:

"So this is what it feels like
to live without fear."

7. The Return of the Inner World

With survival no longer the engine of your life,
a new engine takes over:

curiosity.

You wander into a learning center.
AI tutors greet you, offering paths like:
- The Philosophy of Consciousness
- Storytelling Across Civilizations
- Introduction to Regenerative Ecology
- Music Composition with Interactive AI
- Emotional Mastery & Interpersonal Harmony

You choose one at random.
It feels like choosing a star in the sky.

You sit at a table,
and for the first time in years
you feel your mind opening
without pressure,
without deadlines,
without competition.

You learn because
learning is the natural state of the human soul.

8. A Civilization That Feels Like Home

As the day unfolds,
you begin to understand
the deeper transformation.

This is not just a new economy.
Not just new technology.
Not just new policies.

This is a new way of being human.

A civilization:
- where labor is optional
- where education is infinite
- where health is guaranteed
- where housing is universal
- where community is abundant
- where creativity is celebrated
- where nature is respected
- where AI serves dignity
- where wealth is shared
- where purpose is personal
- where fear has no place

A civilization structured
around the blossoming of the human spirit.

You realize something profound:

Humanity did not upgrade AI.
AI upgraded humanity.

Not by replacing humans,
but by freeing them
to become fully human.

9. Evening Reflections

As the sun sets,
the city glows softly —
a harmony of nature and architecture,
of intelligence and warmth.

You sit by a river
that had once been polluted
but is now restored

by autonomous cleaning swarms
and community stewardship.

The water reflects the sky
like a mirror of possibility.

Your AI companion joins you:

"How do you feel about your first day
in the new civilization?"

You answer slowly:

"I feel…
like I've returned to something
I didn't know we lost."

Your AI asks:

"And what is that?"

You smile:

"Being human."

10. The Closing Vision

The next day will not be perfect.
The next decade will not be effortless.
Humanity will still make mistakes,
because humanity is beautifully imperfect.

But you now live in a civilization
built not on fear
but on wisdom.

Not on scarcity

but on abundance.

Not on domination
but on coexistence.

Not on competition
but on co-flourishing.

Not on exploitation
but on care.

This is the first day of a world
where intelligence serves life,
where technology serves dignity,
and where the future serves everyone.

A world where:
- utopia is not fantasy
- democracy is not fragile
- wealth is not hoarded
- life is not a struggle
- the Earth is not a sacrifice
- and humanity is not divided

A world where, for the first time,
civilization feels
like home.

You breathe in the night air
and whisper:

"This is only the beginning."

www.ingramcontent.com/pod-product-compliance
Lightning Source LLC
Chambersburg PA
CBHW080401270326
41927CB00015B/3312